Morgane Billuart

BECOMING THE PRODUCT

The Critical Internet Researcher as a Virtual Intellectual

TABLE OF CONTENTS

FOREWORD

In 2021, after graduating from art school and wanting to maintain a sense of rigor in my practice and research, I started a podcast entitled "Becoming The Product" where I published research on digital and internet cultures once a month. Although I did not set out on this endeavor with a plan to achieve anything concrete, I did seek to challenge myself to read and produce research beyond my direct remit and share the results eagerly with the world. Shortly before, I had encountered Geert Lovink at the Institute of Network Cultures; around the same time, I discovered the work of Joshua Citarella online. Through these encounters and inspirations, my practice and methods as a researcher started to change and became more speculative, and more experimental, even. Inspired by these two figures, I felt encouraged to actively publish my work and findings online.

The podcast also offered a framework for the creation of a routine to write, research, and archive my readings and findings. Initially envisioned as a project where I would connect personal experiences and daily reflections to broader theories and concepts, the material didn't always appear seamlessly. However, true to my nature and interests, topics often ended up revolving around anything digital: *Chip War and Worldwide Fabs*, *The Phenomenology of the Augmented Life*, *and The Digital Mundane: Risk and Potential*, to name a few. Using concrete examples and theoretical frameworks, I sought to explore fascinating topics with a speculative and experimental approach—not aiming to be "right" or "wrong", but rather to share reflections on the digital and technocratic landscape we navigate every day.

Almost three years later, *Becoming the Product* counts 29 episodes and 116 followers on Soundcloud. That might seem like a disappointing trajectory if measured by metrics alone, but it's a fulfilling one when I consider the dedication and energy that still drives me every time I think about the next topic I want to explore. At times it may be disheartening to realize that the project hasn't taken off to the point where I truly 'became the product'. However, it's also fair to admit that my efforts were not really directed towards that kind of growth: I researched and posted, while never once mentioning payment or asking for recognition—almost as if I were waiting for an angel to descend from the clouds to bless my project.

As an independent writer and researcher, I had already been sustaining critical internet research as a «hobby» for the majority of my adult life. My practice was largely unfunded by neither public nor private patronage. Instead, I took on small, supplementary corporate jobs, which I was fortunate to secure through the gig economy operating on platforms (e.g., Fiverr, Upwork, etc.). Like so many, I have mostly been a precarious researcher producing knowledge online while assuming that critical thinking couldn't provide me with a sufficient income. I willingly took on side jobs and trivial freelance gigs because they allowed me to make a living while creating my creative or critical work in my spare time. These paid projects, though often not the most fascinating, provided me with enough stability and independence to pursue creative and critical endeavors continually. If we lived in an ideal society, things would be different. Opportunities for artists and critical thinkers to fund, develop and deliver their work and theories in less precarious and stressful contexts would be more accessible and evenly distributed. Critical and creative work should not be assumed as free, or in any way a lesser contribution to the economy and functioning societies. As we seem to be hurtling towards an ever more complex world, with right-wing agendas on the rise globally– including in Europe, I believe strongly in the urgency and timeliness of examining models of critical internet research as examples of critical thinking conducted outside of institutional frameworks and regulations and to consider how such work has been sustained over time.

The following essay, along with the interview material included in this book is, however, not about my podcast or my practice. Instead, it is a reflection on the current state of the work of critical internet researchers: their methods, their models, and the questions surrounding the future of their platforms. In this context, the title of my podcast, 'Becoming the Product' offers a framework and a perspective on how researchers can present, benchmark, and adapt their output to remain visible and consumable. At large, this essay contemplates the ever-changing nature of knowledge-making as its frames and forms shapeshift online. Throughout this process, I was fortunate to collaborate with people who not only inspired me but also generously offered me their time and insights as thinkers and researchers, opening perspectives I could not have accessed on my own. With this short preface, I would like to thank Geert Lovink, Sophie Publig, Alex Quicho, Joshua Citarella, Clemens Apprich, Nanna Heidenreich, and Christian Holler for their generosity and support.

INTRODUCTION

In *Digital Plenitude*, Jay David Bolter investigates how contemporary media culture is defined by a vast array of formats and practices, driven by two major shifts that occurred in the last fifty years: the decline of elitism in the arts and the simultaneous rise of digital media. In the opening pages of his book, the theorist discusses two significant developments that have transformed our understanding of culture and art: the emergence of digital media and the decline of our collective belief in what might be termed "Culture with a Capital C."[1] These shifts, which he argues began in the 1970s and 1990s, continue their trajectory today, having already fractured the once-assumed hierarchy of knowledge and taste. Released from hierarchical judgments of taste, enjoyers of symphonies may co-mingle easily with those who prefer reggae; some delve into classic literature while others are drawn to films, writes Boulter.[2] As these boundaries and differences gradually dissolved, universities and researchers began to explore the various ways that digital media, its production, and its impacts started intersecting increasingly with daily life, highlighting its profound influence on both the creation and analysis of culture. Digital media and its platforms propelled the collapse of hierarchies of culture and became a field of research and inquiry in its own right.

As the web expanded and digital cultures became more pervasive, individual researchers and entire media departments began examining its developments, seeking to establish analytical, strategical, and critical discourses around it. With the increasing popularity of internet and digital advancements, 'critical internet research'[3]—a specialized

1.   Jay David Bolter, *The Digital Plenitude : The Decline of Elite Culture and the Rise of New Media* (The MIT Press, 2019), 1.
2.   Bolter, *The Digital Plenitude*, 11.
3.   As introduced in the interview and conversation with Geert Lovink.

field within the study of digital cultures—has garnered increasing attention over the years for its critical, investigative, and experimental approach. These practices did not merely emerge when a few individuals started highlighting the downsides of the internet's growth; rather, they stem from a continuous and universal tradition of critical and political scrutiny of the World Wide Web, its economic models, and its societal impact.[4] Alternative and speculative, the tone and genre of critical internet research have often appeared on the margins of research-making, frequently mutating through and with the internet.

To illuminate the field of critical internet research, its origins, and its challenges, this essay focuses on two pivotal figures: Geert Lovink and Joshua Citarella. Despite their differing approaches, shaped by generational, national, and political influences, the study examines how Lovink and Citarella built communities centered on internet theory and its critique. Building on Jay David Bolter's argument in *Digital Plenitude*, this essay examines the rise of digital cultures and the commodification of knowledge within the context of critical internet research, underlying the strategies employed by intellectuals and artists to promote and showcase their analysis on digital platforms. The key figures within this research—Geert Lovink, Joshua Citarella, and the archetypal Theory Girl— will be analyzed through the lens of the 'Virtual Intellectual', a concept introduced by Geert Lovink in 1997.[5] Through this lineage, I aim to provide insights into critical internet research and highlight how it proliferates by adapting to shifting ideologies, economic conditions, and platform incentives.

4.   Jeremy Hunsinger, Matthew M.Allen, and Lisbeth Klastrup, eds., *Second International Handbook of Internet Research* (Springer, 2020), 398.

5.   Geert Lovink, "Portrait of the Virtual Intellectual," mailing list, *Nettime* (blog), July 20, 1997, https://nettime.org/Lists−Archives/nettime−l−9707/msg00065.html.

Indeed, while the 1990s and 2000s were characterized by distinct collective and activist critical research, this essay will outline more recent and market-oriented strategies for sustaining internet criticism today.

While discussing the various initiatives within critical internet research, the following essay does not seek to impose a strict binary distinction between institutional and non-institutional, individualist and collective approaches, nor between private and public funding sources. While such distinctions often provide a convenient lens for understanding the world, this research aims to demonstrate that the most effective models blend elements and polarities, while striving for a balanced and integrated approach. Institutions rely on the critical perspectives of both individuals and grassroots movements, just as much as the latter depends upon the support and structure that institutions may provide. Particularly in the European context, the growing influence of right-wing politics in countries where state funding once played a pivotal role in supporting art, alternative practices, and critical thought is crucial to acknowledge when considering these less-than-simple dependencies and relationships. Amid funding cuts and the privatization of previously public models, thinkers, creators, and operators of independent spaces are compelled to rethink their strategies to sustain their work. In this context, critical internet research holds particular significance as a case study of a field that has frequently and historically depended on self-organization and developed beyond the confines of traditional institutions. Indeed, given the interdisciplinary nature of this field of research, internet researchers often had to chart their own paths, championing topics and ideas that may appear niche or unconventional but often resonate with audiences outside of mainstream channels.

As critical researchers, media theorist Geert Lovink and visual artist Joshua Citarella were tactical pioneers, as they decided to post their research online, and taking on the internet and technology not only as a subject of study but also as a method to distribute research. Although this research mostly focuses on these two figures, it is also important to note that many other thinkers, including women and non-white individuals, are contributing to this field of research. To name just a few: Kidology, Internet Analysis, and Emily Segal are other figures of study that illustrate this phenomenon well, enlightening us on how the concept of the 'Theory Girl' can come to life online through aesthetics and performativity. While these figures aren't the first object of analysis, their work most definitely inspired this research.

I will begin with a concise overview of Geert Lovink's work in the 1990s, highlighting his research and initiatives that addressed fundamental questions about the future of internet research and laid the groundwork for the establishment of the Institute of Network Cultures. I'll then consider how Joshua Citarella's community-building efforts, particularly through his platform *Do Not Research*, continue these critical inquiries in adventurous ways, as the artist and his community endlessly navigate "the Dark Forest of the Internet"[6] with plenty of hybris. While questioning the ideal of the self-organized critical entrepreneur, this work simultaneously argues that strategic and aesthetic approaches may need to be structured for the critical internet researcher to endure and sustain their practice. Examining the various strategies and performativities surrounding the archetype of the virtual intellectual, I will evaluate the limitations of critical internet research

14

6. Yancey Strickler, Venkatesh Rao, and Maggie Appleton, The Dark Forest Anthology of the Internet (*The Dark Forest Collective*, n.d.), accessed December 22, 2024.

taking place online and explore the figure of the "Theory Girl" as a producer of online discourse and its aesthetics. Finally, this work will address questions and concerns surrounding the future of the figure of the critical internet researcher, their economic sustainability and viability beyond platforms through interviews with Gert Lovink, Joshua Citarella, Alex Quicho, and Sophie Publig.

Finally, before we dive in, it is important to first clarify the terminologies used throughout this essay. The concepts of internet studies and digital cultures are often intermixed, a confusion and tension that mirrors broader debates within the fields of media studies and digital cultures. Therefore, the terminology used in this research presents an interesting challenge. For the sake of clarity, I have chosen to adopt the definition of 'critical internet research' proposed by Geert Lovink,[7] and occasionally refer to the term 'Internet criticism', as it is used by Joshua Citarella in his terms.[8] In terms of its scope, critical internet research is narrower than 'media studies' and more focused than 'digital cultures', which carries theoretical and methodological weight in academic discourse. Critical internet research aims to interpret the internet and digital culture critically and speculatively, engaging with associations and ideas that may emerge spontaneously and faster than traditional academic processes may allow. As such, the critical internet researcher's work extends beyond formats native to peer-reviewed journals and academic articles. They may choose to practice speculative and experimental explorations,[9] all while investigating internet and digital

7.   As introduced in conversations with Geert Lovink and throughout the interview.
8.   'Joshua Citarella', Accessed 19 December 2024, http://joshuacitarella.com/cv.html.
9.   Jeremy Hunsinger, Matthew M.Allen, and Lisbeth Klastrup, eds., *Second International Handbook of Internet Research* (Springer, 2020), 6.

culture, including its platforms, users, and artifacts, as well as economic, political, and societal implications.[10] Furthermore, I will use the term 'virtual intellectual,' via a definition put forth by Geert Lovink,[11] which will be later introduced and referred to throughout this essay. While the concept of the virtual intellectual can be applied and studied beyond the field of critical internet research (e.g., in politics, philosophy, etc.), this book primarily focuses on its manifestations within critical internet research specifically.

10. Hunsinger, M.Allen and Klastrup, *Second International Handbook of Internet Research*, 396–398.
11. Geert Lovink, *Dark Fiber: Tracking Critical Internet Culture* (The MIT Press, 2003), 55.

THE EVER-CHANGING STATUS OF INTERNET STUDIES

The Case of Critical Internet Research

Both online and offline, the initial allure of the web and its promises of endless possibilities for personal freedom and expanded creativity has drawn significant scrutiny, mired by suspicions about its trajectory and consequences. As *The Handbook of Internet Studies* expounds, researchers were slow but sure to adapt to the internet's rapid development by setting up the field of media studies and critical research centers at various universities.[12] In its early days, the internet primarily offered text-based content as objects of research. However, it grew rapidly and expanded its applications and mediums, soon providing users and researchers with a wide range of experiences, from images to games and emails to instant chats. As the internet expanded further from static monitors to mobile phones, from the desktop to various settings of everyday life, leading platforms, and digital ecosystems to infiltrate our routines and habits, researchers continually sought to understand their scope and implications, whether through institutional or alternative channels. Throughout the years, research centers, academic programs, and online communities were built simultaneously, driven by a desire to better understand how human beings learned to communicate and share knowledge over the web.[13]

12. Mia Consalvo and Charles Ess, eds., *The Handbook of Internet Studies* (Blackwell Publishing, 2011), 7.
13. Consalvo and Ess, *The Handbook of Internet Studies*, 8.

Within its introduction, *The Handbook of Internet Studies* highlights that the relatively recent incorporation of digital studies and media theory departments within academia represents an effort to create a coherent body of knowledge in response to the fast-moving and ever-evolving landscape of internet theory and digital culture. Over time, various attempts and research projects have been undertaken to better analyze and study the internet and its development, contributing to the growth and legitimization of the discipline.

In 2013, Richard Rogers put forth *Digital Methods*, one of many renowned academic strategies adopted by media studies departments, educational settings, and research centers. In his eponymous book, Rogers discusses the challenges of studying the internet as a medium, noting its transient and changeful nature. To support the study of the Internet as a distinct field within the social sciences, he advocates for new methods of analysis, such as incorporating computational techniques to capture and analyze hyperlinks, tags, and search engines. This "rework [of] methods for Internet-related research" would develop "a novel strand of study, digital methods."[14] The relevance of this rework and focus was highlighted by the fact that the internet had already become a site of research far beyond online culture, serving as the focus of inquiry and findings for a much broader field than media studies alone, argues Rogers.[15] As such, *Digital Methods* serves as a valuable contribution to the foundation of internet studies, offering an academically rigorous framework for researching both the internet itself and using it as a research engine and tool.

However, leveraging the internet for theory-making raises several challenges. These include questions regarding the reliability of sources, the variability and volatility of

14. Richard Rogers, *Digital Methods* (The MIT Press, 2013), 31.
15. Rogers, *Digital Methods*, 35.

platforms, and the demand for swift responses from online audiences. Furthermore, this domain of research is inherently tied to a new paradigm of learning and practice—one that is deeply rooted in cross-disciplinarity. As underlined in the *Second International Handbook of Internet Research,* "Internet studies also might research politics, political economy, cultures, subcultures, the socius related to any of the internets such as dark web communities, Reddit users, /b/, Amazon, Twitch, Second Life, or innumerable others. Race, gender, ethnicity, and similar are also engaging topics of internet studies. Feminist studies are significant in the field of internet studies, as are LGBTQ studies."[16] Indeed, internet theory and digital cultures necessitate a fusion of multiple disciplines to make sense of emerging phenomena, rendering their methodologies and analyses both opaque and experimental.[17] Over the years, this field of study has continued to expand and evolve, incorporating an ever-growing range of disciplines such as politics, economics, and aesthetics, all of which, when combined, "make for a massively complex and broad field of study."[18] Therefore, internet studies and their critical inquiries face the challenge of being dismissed for being not scientifically rigorous enough, too biased, and empirical. Despite their limitations, media studies and digital culture programs have certainly thrived within art schools and universities,[19] a growth indicating a recognized necessity to educate young people and future generations about these subjects.

16.   Jeremy Hunsinger, Matthew M.Allen, and Lisbeth Klastrup, eds., Second International Handbook of Internet Research (Springer, 2020), 386.

17.   Hunsinger, M.Allen and Klastrup, *Second International Handbook of Internet Research,* 14.

18.   Hunsinger, M.Allen and Klastrup, *Second International Handbook of Internet Research,* 398.

19.   Hunsinger, M.Allen and Klastrup, *Second International Handbook of Internet Research,* 409.

While academics debated the most effective analytical tools and focused on defining the boundaries of social sciences and the humanities, critical internet research—a parallel field of inquiry and practice— thrived in mailing lists and network initiatives. The involved researchers, who relied on alternative methods and speculative models to strengthen their arguments, saw the public's reception of their work–which could easily be hosted online,t hriving outside of academic circles.[20] The proliferation of independent internet researchers including Geert Lovink, Pit Schultz, and later on, the Youtubers Internet Analysis, Kidology, or internet critic Joshua Citarella, demonstrate the growing success of alternative presentation models in internet research and digital cultures at large. With or without the backing of academic institutions, these thinkers developed and adapted diverse strategies and economic models, becoming reliant on audience engagement and direct support via newsletters or mailing lists for the proliferation of their work, while sustaining themselves financially via diverse revenue streams.

The continuous effort and opportunity to conduct and publish critical internet research via alternative platforms has brought both benefits and challenges to the broader field of internet and media theory. On the one hand, researchers who publish on YouTube, Spotify, or Substack seem to be able to reach audiences of thousands or even hundreds of thousands, far exceeding the limited readership of academic papers. Consequently, this democratization may dilute rigorous research, reducing it to a matter of opinions that could, lack the depth and precision characteristic of traditional scholarly work. The field of internet

20. This reflection is based on the number of views, reach, or audience engagement that the theorists and commentators mentioned have achieved when sharing their research online–figures that significantly surpass the average view count of an academic article.

studies continuously grapples with this challenge. By disseminating their work via these platforms, researchers navigate the gray area between influencers and academic researchers, with their work emphasizing the challenge of making their theory both accessible and engaging for a broad audience. These efforts help foster critical thinking in a world where platforms and companies evolve faster than policy-making and academic research in institutions can respond. Let's take a closer look at the foundational practices of early critical internet researchers. Which figures played a central role in the development of this nascent field? Which framework supports the role of the critical internet researcher as a virtual intellectual, marked by experimental efforts to maintain their recognition online?

Early Net Criticism and the Work of Geert Lovink

Geert Lovink stands as a prominent figure and early champion of speculative and non-traditional academic approaches for those exploring internet theory and criticism. Born in 1959 in Amsterdam, Geert's life work focuses on a detailed examination of internet and platform developments, which was partly conducted independently or outside of institutional contexts. He is in leadership of the Institute of Network Cultures (also known as 'INC'), which has produced countless books and conferences. The institute fosters internet and technological criticism, nurturing a collaborative and critical environment in which numerous employees and affiliated researchers have conducted internet criticism beyond traditional academic frameworks.[21] As an activist and theoretician in the making, one of Geert Lovink's early missions was to study computer networks and their implications beyond the context of technological development, arguing that technological standards should urgently become a site of political and economic reflection.[22] In his book *Dark Fiber*, published in 2002, he already makes his intention very clear: "This study has the Internet as its natural environment."[23]

21. "Institute of Network Cultures," organisation, Monoskop (blog), May 19, 2015, https://monoskop.org/Institute_of_Network_Cultures.
22. Geert Lovink, Dark Fiber: Tracking Critical Internet Culture (The MIT Press, 2003), 21.
23. Lovink, Dark Fiber, 14.

Beyond viewing the internet as a potential market for speculative growth and a showcase of human desires and propositions, Geert Lovink, from the outset of his career, argued that internet studies should be approached from all possible angles: its content, forms, technologies, and users.[24] Focusing on a "critical techno-culture", he is one of the key figures suggesting that such an inquiry should not be exclusive or limited, but instead, expand its horizons.[25] His arguments for the development of critical internet research were often grounded in a critique of the limitations and strict boundaries of scope within academic disciplinary approaches that would dissect internet studies "as if society and technology can still be separated."[26] However, according to the theorist's forecast, this was bound to change. Geert Lovink foresaw the rigidity of German media theory as unsuitable for a medium that would move too fast, thereby requiring a more speculative approach. In the 1990s, he was already envisioning how future public figures and internet critics would need to transfer critical knowledge into networks, potentially moving away from traditional media reputation systems to be heard and recognized publicly.

In 1997, Geert coined the terminology of the 'Internet Critical Influencer', which is expanded upon in the chapter "The Portrait of the Virtual Intellectual" of his book, *Dark Fiber*. As such, one could argue that Geert predicted the gradual decline of intellectuals as distant, idolized figures, foreseeing a shift where they would have to confront and navigate the dominance and overwhelming presence of new digital media. He envisioned the figure of a reckless researcher, one who "will no longer accept the editorial tyranny of the Gutenberg bosses."[27] Existing beyond

24.   Lovink, *Dark Fiber*, 26.
25.   Lovink, *Dark Fiber*, 29.
26.   Lovink, *Dark Fiber*, 31.

the remit of academia, with its support and institutional backing, Lovink suggested that such an individual would have their own website and revenue model, consisting of a string of micro-payments and self-organized structures. But perhaps other than a Youtuber or a Twitch streamer, Geert Lovink envisioned an individual who could exist and research post-media platforms, and which would always be under construction. While the concept of the virtual intellectual is only one of many contributions arising from the theorist's prolific practice and career, we can see his theories unfold in real-time through his own achievements and efforts to build networks beyond traditional institutions. Through initiatives like the Amsterdam Digital City and the Nettime mailing list, Lovink, along with his colleagues and peers, remained consistently focused on media and internet criticism on digital platforms, hoping these channels would stay free and accessible indefinitely.

Nettime, as mentioned in *Dark Fiber*, was a mailing list created in 1995-1996. It has become widely recognized as one of the leading forums "for the discussion and practice of innovative Internet culture and Internet-based art"[28] by consistently pondering the question: "What might Internet criticism in the digital age look like?" Over the years, the mailing list, which was voluntarily and freely moderated, endured due to a few individuals' firm belief and dedication, including Pit Schultz, Ted Byfield, and Felix Stalder. The question of the organizational model of such a platform, as well as the degrees of freedom set by the moderator were constantly renegotiated, but the urgent pursuit of a sustainable model floated the description and historical timeline of the project consistently. In this context, the conditions for the project's sustainability not only meant

27. Geert Lovink, *Dark Fiber: Tracking Critical Internet Culture* (The MIT Press, 2003), 55.
28. Lovink, *Dark Fiber*, 86.

free content but also concerned its organization and maintenance, given that all moderators always participated for free: "What are the economics of list culture? Even with a web archive, email lists hardly generate traffic. While running at virtually no cost, like most virtual communities building up and maintaining a list is time-consuming work, done by volunteers."[29] Geert Lovink's involvement in the early critical development of the web extended beyond the screen; his efforts were not only documented online but also manifested offline, in events and conferences such as Metaforum, Fiber Culture, among others. These days, many explorations and organizations supported or initiated by Geert Lovink remain: the Nettime newsletter is still active, Metaforum conferences continue to take place occasionally, and books on internet analysis and criticism are continuously published by the Institute of Network Cultures.

An examination of Geert's mission to legitimize critical internet research would be amiss without mentioning the foundation and development of the Institute of Network Cultures over the years. Although this host and producer of events, publications and dialogue located in Amsterdam is an institutional entity, its unique positioning helps us understand how critical internet research can persist and continue to be supported through educational and state-funded resources. Supported by the Amsterdam University of Applied Sciences, the institute has weathered challenges over the years by identifying itself as a research center within an applied arts university.[30] Although this institutional affiliation involves diplomatic and political complexities, it is important to note that this support has played a key role in the institute's resilience and longevity. The argument developed here does not

29. Lovink, *Dark Fiber*, 115.
30. "Institute of Network Cultures," organisation, *Monoskop* (blog), May 19, 2015, https://monoskop.org/Institute_of_Network_Cultures.

particularly suggest that the development and growth of the institute could not have been sustained without the support of a structural institution. Geert's practice and dedication, long before the institute was established, clearly showed that his commitment and activism went far beyond the pursuit of institutional funding or a paid teaching position. Like many others, he had to fund his efforts while continuing his work.

The issue of economics on the internet and the various strategies to sustain digital practices has often been a central focus of Geert Lovink's work which in turn has informed the agenda of the Institute of Network Cultures. In the Youtube video *Geert Lovink: A Short History of MoneyLab,* he retraces the history of money on the internet and with the internet, a wonder that started with the birth of the internet payment system in 1992. MoneyLab, which began in 2014, was a research project that included conferences and publications with rather diverse agendas: crowdfunding, monetization, financialization, Bitcoin,... the list of endeavors was endless and expanded as the internet proposed different mechanisms and strategies over time.[31] For internet artists and critics within this sphere, there was a profound understanding of the need to question the strategies and possibilities for monetizing content in the era of digital culture. Although Geert Lovink foretold the arrival of the virtual intellectual as a figure and was theorizing how such an individual could monetize their practice, it is relevant to notice that the theorist was himself reluctant to use GAFAs (Google, Apple, Facebook et Amazon) platforms.[32]

31. *Geert Lovink: A Short History of MoneyLab,* Youtube link, 2023, https://www.youtube.com/watch?v=WIaeWqmyqTE.
32. Geert Lovink, "Join the Facebook Exodus on May 31!" Blog, *Institute of Network Cultures* (blog), May 27, 2010, https://networkcultures.org/geert/2010/05/27/join-the-face-book-exodus-on-may-31/.

This did not impact the reputation of the theorist nor the INC, which, thanks to the team's motivation and institutional funding, successfully produced conference after conference and publication after publication, all without the mediated support of platforms like Facebook, Instagram, TikTok, YouTube, or others. However, other critical internet researchers would need to employ a variety of strategies to be visible and remain attractive, therefore it is clear that the model of the INC was unique in this regard.

Joshua Citarella: Internet Criticism on Social Media

At first glance, it might seem odd to introduce Joshua Citarella as a continuous figure taking on the baton from Geert Lovink. However, among others, Joshua Citarella's practice is exemplary of the virtual intellectual Geert Lovink foresaw coming. Not only does he study the internet, but he also produces and shares his findings using methods that align with the aesthetics and forms native to the medium. Sometimes he even tailors these to the given audience in an effort to deliberately demonstrate how aesthetics and politics work hand in hand. Additionally, Joshua's experiments with agility across crowdfunding and micro-payment systems make him a figure who, although not immune to criticism, can be said to study, use, and benefit from the internet in multifaceted ways.

As mentioned on his website, Joshua Citarella, born in 1987 in New York, is an artist and writer known for his exploration of internet culture and online communities.[33] He studied at the School of Visual Arts in New York, where his education bridged traditional photography and emerging digital methods, reflecting the institution's shift in focus during his educational time. This dual foundation informs his work, which often examines the intersections of technology, art, and contemporary online phenomena.

33. 'Joshua Citarella', Accessed 19 December 2024, http://joshuacitarella.com/cv.html.

He hosts the Doomscroll podcast and initiated the online platform *Do Not Research*, which delves into the dynamics of digital subcultures since 2020. In 2019, Citarella announced that he would quit his teaching position at the Rhode Island School of Design to share his research through an online syllabus, purchasable for the accessible price of 5$ per month. The artist and theorist was not only encouraging his audience to support his research but he was also implying that the traditional educational path and the art market were becoming obsolete.[34] He seemed to be suggesting that brighter opportunities awaited those who chose to deviate from a conventional artistic trajectory. It appeared as though his post was ushering in a future where institutions and academia could soon collapse.

In the later published essay, *We Need New Platforms To Tell New Stories,* Joshua Citarella recalls the decisive moments that pushed him away from teaching to start his career as a content creator instead: "This September, I'm not going back to teaching. I've spent the past few years arguing against the idea that online platforms could be a suitable replacement for institutions. But now, I'm leaving my university jobs to become a content creator."[35] As explained in his text, Joshua's decision to withdraw wasn't solely driven by a sense of marginalization, but rather by his realization of the impossibility of creating works and reflections on objects that could challenge the status quo of private collections and institutional funding: "the donor class will not facilitate critiques of their real power."[36] While Joshua's case is unique, I suggest that his

34.   Yancey Strickler, Venkatesh Rao, and Maggie Appleton,
      The Dark Forest Anthology of the Internet
      (The Dark Forest Collective, n.d.), 65.
35.   Yancey Strickler, Venkatesh Rao, and Maggie Appleton,
      The Dark Forest Anthology of the Internet
      (The Dark Forest Collective, n.d.), 65.
36.   Strickler, *The Dark Forest Anthology of the Internet*, 66.

case is perfectly relevant to our argument as the artist studied subcultures and extreme politics in the first place. Therefore, one would not have been amiss to assume that perhaps his community and readership could be found elsewhere than in grand halls and white cubes. In his essay, the artist finally concludes by arguing that artists or thinkers as we used to know and adore them, no longer exist as a professional class, and that the privilege to engage with complex ideas has to be grasped via different strategies in order to adapt.

A few years later, Joshua, who decided to fully embrace this new path, now has over 60,000 followers on Instagram. He has developed content streams for publications and research that extend far beyond his practice. A prominent example of his organizational and publishing efforts is the *Do Not Research* Substack, where the artist, alongside other moderators, republishes weekly news articles, artworks, and essays on digital and internet culture. Far removed from the safety of institutional funding and distinct from a traditional art magazine, *Do Not Research* is a subscription-based platform that supports the propagation of works and ideas aligned with critical and speculative theory.[37] Whereas Joshua Citarella's practice began within institutional frameworks before transitioning toward greater independence, Geert Lovink's practice was self-initiated long before its institutionalization. Nevertheless, as previously argued, framing the discussion in terms of dichotomies such as institutional versus self-funding or private versus public proves unproductive for the aims of this essay. What can be assessed, rather, are the multiple approaches that emerge in practicing and producing critical internet research, along with the various possibilities for sustaining these practices.

37. "Do Not Research," Substack, Do Not Research, December 22, 2024, https://donotresearch.substack.com/.

Figures like Joshua Citarella have pursued projects and publishing practices that emphasize how the rise of platforms and the concept of the thinker-influencer are deliberate responses to the limitations of traditional formats and imposed forms for thinking and creating. As previously argued, older or more conservative models struggled to accommodate the speculative and experimental approaches required by the internet, digital research and its agents. This tension, which can be traced back to Geert Lovink's early theories and concerns, is now manifesting in increasingly defined ways through the emergence and establishment of the virtual intellectual as a figure. In the conversation *Memes vs. Museums: Joshua Citarella, Dena Yago, Cem A., G. Quack – The Future of Critique (18.11.22),* Joshua Citarella evokes an analogy between the New York Times and Substack, emphasizing that there exists, indeed, a drift from legacy institutions towards alternative forms of media. As discussed during the panel, the simplistic dichotomy between institutions and platforms, or individuals and institutions—in this case, the museum—is insufficient. Both Citarella and the researcher Dena Yago explain that while they operate within platform-based spaces, their established reputations enable them to continue engaging with institutions and, in some cases, even corporations.

In this 'Digital Plenitude', where mainstream cultures and subcultures emerge and intertwine, where ad revenue and micro-payments thrive, and which Yancey Strickler has coined 'The Dark Forest of the Internet,' thinkers and creators must learn to navigate its diverse terrains, determining how to best present their persona, their research, and the most effective ways to sustain them. In the edited volume, *The Dark Forest Anthology of the Internet,* written and edited by the Dark Forest Collective, artist Joshua Citarella narrates once again his decision to leave the confines of academia to enter and embrace this 'Dark Forest'.[38] Nevertheless, he caveats: "We cannot say where this is going. We can only say where we've been. Welcome to the Dark Forest Anthology of the Internet."[39] Throughout the volume various contributors discuss methodologies and models of payment, calling overall for a detachment from mainstream channels and further efforts to create new ones. However, as we will later highlight, detaching from such platforms is an opportunity only a few well-established and highly reputed individuals can afford.

38. Yancey Strickler, Venkatesh Rao, and Maggie Appleton,
     The Dark Forest Anthology of the Internet (The Dark Forest
     Collective, n.d.), 8.
39. Strickler, Rao, and Appleton, *The Dark Forest Anthology
     of the Internet,* 10.

Critical Internet Research:
From the Institute of Network Culture
to Do Not Research

At first glance, it may appear incongruous to compare two markedly different initiatives: The Institute of Network Cultures, established in the early 2000s within the context of an applied sciences institution, and the other: *Do Not Research*, emerging around 2020, sustained entirely through micro-payment systems and subscription-based models. The purpose of this essay is not to establish rigid parallels or direct comparisons between these two examples but rather to examine how critical internet research has been explored and rendered visible in the online sphere. Moreover, with the impending retirement of Geert Lovink and the accompanying questions surrounding the sustainability of the Institute of Network Cultures, issues of legacy, continuity, and economic viability are brought to the forefront. Returning to a comparison, the subjects of research for Joshua Citarella and Geert Lovink differ: while they may both focus on the internet and its cultures, their subjects of expertise and interests are not the same. While we may not be able to compare or mirror these two figures directly, we can position their respective initiatives within the broader timeline of critical internet research and its evolving models of existence and publication.

Since its inception, the Institute of Network Cultures (INC) has established itself as an online platform for hosting critical reflections on technology, producing more speculative and experimental research than traditional academic papers. By regularly hosting blog posts and publishing articles on internet culture and its politics, the Institute of Network Cultures established itself as a unique institution—one that attracted numerous researchers and fellows seeking to engage in critical internet research beyond the confines of academia. On its website, the platform introduces itself as an institute that explores and influences the landscape of network cultures through events, publications, and online discussions.[40] Its projects focus on topics such as urgent publishing, alternative revenue models, critical design and creation, digital counterculture, and more.[41] Founded in 2004 by Geert Lovink after his appointment at the Amsterdam University of Applied Sciences, the INC emphasizes building sustainable research networks. It identifies and practically addresses emerging critical issues. Following an interdisciplinary approach, the INC connects researchers, artists, activists, programmers, designers, students, and educators. On its webpage, the INC presents published research, announcements for events, archives of past events and productions, as well as blog posts. As a matter of example and possible illustration, these are some recently published articles on the platform at the current time of writing: "Youmaxxing – Masculinity and the Online Self-Improvement Culture" by Francesco Barchiesi, "Memes as a Portal to the Past and Future: How Extinction Rebellion Is Using Memes to Change the Narrative Around the Climate Crisis" by Chloe Arkenbout, or "The Kawayoku Tales:

40. As read on 'Institute of Network Cultures',
    Accessed 19 December 2024, https://networkcultures.org/.
41. As read on 'Institute of Network Cultures',
    Accessed 19 December 2024, https://networkcultures.org/.
42. As read on 'Institute of Network Cultures',
    Accessed 19 December 2024, https://networkcultures.org/.

Aestheticisation of Violence in Military, Gaming, Social Media Cultures and Other Stories" by Noura Tefeche.[42]

Do Not Research (DNR) was founded in 2020 as a private *Discord* server to explore memetic propagation and the internet's role in shaping political trends. Over time, it evolved into a publishing platform for writing, visual art, internet culture research, and more.[43] Operating independently from institutional funding, *Do Not Research* relies on the voluntary work of its moderators and structures its content around open call-based submissions that offer a small payment for contributors. Originally hosted on a website, *Do Not Research* now primarily runs through Substack, where readers can contribute financially to access exclusive content and join a Discord community. Each year, the platform launches an open call for new articles and productions which end up being selected and printed in yearly editions. On the *Do Not Research* webpage, visitors can scroll through art reviews, announcements, and theoretical texts that explore similar subjects and maintain a tone akin to that of the Institute of Network Cultures. On the main page, one can find a myriad of fascinating articles, such as "The Dialectic of Doomscrolling" by Kat Kitay, "Digital Ruination and the Memetic Lifecycle" by Isabella Haid, or "Enduring AI Power Structures: Nuance and System Fragility" by Alexandra Gilliams.[44] DNR has, within just a few years, established itself as a reference platform for digital and internet discourse, enabling young researchers to not only publish research that could not be hosted elsewhere but also to gravitate toward a community of artists and researchers concerned with similar issues.

43. As read on 'Institute of Network Cultures', Accessed 19 December 2024, https://networkcultures.org/.
44. As read on "Do Not Research," Substack, Do Not Research, December 22, 2024, https://donotresearch.substack.com/.

The Institute of Network Cultures and *Do Not Research* appear to share a similar mission and vision. Their aesthetics and tones, in contrast to the neutrality often found in academic journals, are thoughtfully crafted, with a distinctive focus on the design of their platforms and articles, ensuring a unique and engaging presentation. Additionally, both platforms rely primarily on submissions from internal and external participants. However, *Do Not Research* stands out as a compelling example of an independent platform as it operates without relying on institutional or state funding, but rather, on a subscription model. This independence highlights its significance as a case study, demonstrating how self-organized, community-based efforts can sustain speculative and critical thinking. In this context, *Do Not Research* introduces a format that could be valuable for further exploration regarding the economic and operational sustainability of independent para-institutional research online.

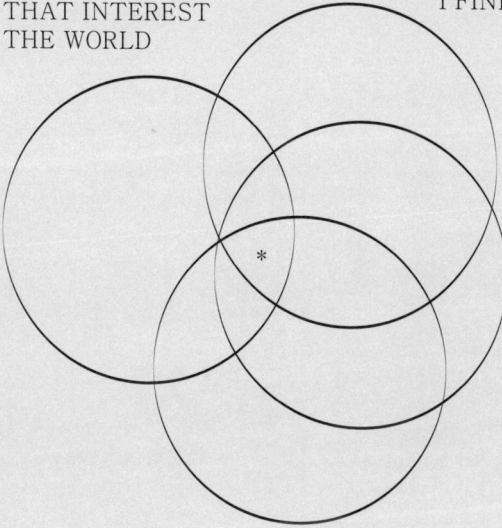

ONLINE THINGS
THAT INTEREST
THE WORLD

ONLINE THINGS
I FIND INTERESTING

CATCHY
HEADLINES
AND VISUALS

THEORETICAL FRAMEWORK WITH
A SPECULATIVE APPROACH

* QUALITATIVE DELIVERY OF CRITICAL INTERNET RESEARCH

THE IDEAL
OF THE
SELF−ORGANISED
CRITICAL
INTERNET
RESEARCHER

On Patronage and Precarity

Many would argue that the self-employed, self-made, self-organized researcher in an ever-growing capitalist world should not be the answer to our curses. Idolizing a self-managed and self-oriented career or business while institutions fail to support us may seem, for some, like the simplest way to withdraw from politics and accountability. As such, 'becoming a product', i.e. conceiving of one's practice as a business model, is perhaps the response most aligned with a neoliberalist fate instead of seeing one revolt and manifest a better and well-distributed system. Additionally, the life of an entrepreneur or CEO, while appearing glamorous and stylish in many business areas, isn't as lucrative and shimmering as it may seem. While a lucky few may find success on Substack and other channels, it is not a sustainable and wishful model for widespread adoption. Many theorists and artists have criticized this "economy of the self" with which they have found themselves stuck or eternally struggling with.[45] As previously mentioned, in the best possible world, everyone would indeed benefit from a better, more well-funded, and reliable system instead of feeling as if they existed in the never-ending rat race for the next gig, the next viral video, amplified by the pressures and whims of the algorithm. However, the concept of a self-sustaining practice fueled by patronage is not entirely new.

45. Silvio Lorusso, Entreprecariat (Onomatopee, 2019), 10.

Pursuing a career as an intellectual or artist has historically been characterized by limited financial profitability.
The stereotype of the solitary, struggling, and financially
strained artist is deeply ingrained, and frequently portrayed as an archetype in books and movies. The notion
of cultural and artistic work as a site of struggle persists
throughout history. While this trope holds true for many,
as institutional funding or non-monetary support often remains limited, we may, for the sake of this argument, turn
towards a wealth of strategies and leveraged opportunities that creatives have historically employed to sustain
their practices. In the book *Art Worlds* by Howard Becker,
the sociologist emphasizes from the first pages that despite the pervasive myth of the artist as a misunderstood
genius and lone wolf, they always exist within the "collective activity we can call an art world."[46] While different
projects call for various amounts of concrete or symbolic
capital in support, the discreteness of the artist as an individual becomes blurred by such dependencies argues
Becker. As early as 1982, long before the rise of entrepreneurship and the self-made online freelancer, Howard
emphasized that the reputation of an artist should be their
central focus, especially for those attempting to operate
outside of traditional channels.[47]

   While Howard Becker mostly illustrates the art world
and its dynamics in this book, many parallels can be made
between this field of inquiry and critical internet research.
Indeed, there exist parallels between Joshua Citarella's
declaration of the failures of the creative system and the
early analysis of Howard Becker. As stated in the early
pages of his book, the sociologist emphasizes the increasing number of students willing to attend art school in the

46. Howard Becker, *Art Worlds* University of California Press,
    1982), 1.
47. Becker, *Art Worlds*, 25.

USA, followed by the sobering number of those who can "make it" professionally: "No art has sufficient resources to support economically or give sympathetic attention to all or any substantial proportion of those trainees in the way customary in the art worlds for which they are being trained. This is an important proviso. If the arts were organized differently— less professional, less star-oriented, less centralized—that support might be available."[48] With the increasing cost of education and the increased cut of public funding worldwide, one can only imagine the urgency of dealing with such a topic today. What will happen to art-making, experimentation, and critical thinking if state funding is gradually withdrawn from the spaces that previously fostered creativity and connections? In an increasingly privatized educational landscape, who will have the capacity and privilege to create, innovate, and cultivate critical thinking?

The struggles faced by those individuals and collectives are no novelty, with considerations of survival strategies already being introduced and analyzed within the framework of Howard Becker, who argued that in a precarious freelance system, the question of reputation was of the utmost importance.[49] In such a competitive and limited industry, professionally marginal artists or thinkers must secure their platform and, to the extent of possibility, ensure that their work is distributed. The question of reputation, network, and distribution does not apply to the ones who can already finance their work and do not need to consider such assets.[50] Nowadays, the latter might be referred to as nepo-baby,[51] a popular

48. Becker, *Art Worlds*, 52.
49. Becker, *Art Worlds*, 86.
50. Becker, *Art Worlds*, 110.
51. The term "nepo baby" is a colloquial expression referring to individuals who achieve success or gain opportunities in their field primarily due to familial connections, often in entertainment, media, or other high-profile industries.

vernacular phrase for the already successful or privileged individual who may choose the luxury of remaining private or anonymous since influence is already abundant in their milieu and repertoire. An advantage that only a few possess, and which we will question at a later moment. Individuals and artists who have found institutional constraints too rigid have always sought ways to exist outside of their boundaries. Consider the example of the *Salon des Refusés*,[52] for instance, which demonstrates that those who reject established models often pave the way for significant reconsiderations of artistic practices and their hegemonies.

Becker describes the concept of a patronage system as: "some person or organization supports the artist entirely for a period during which the artist contracts to produce specific works or a specified number of works, or even just possibly to produce some works."[53] This dynamic, which has existed for centuries, was often initiated by wealthy individuals who could dictate and commission specific works from an artist, whether a painting, a piece of music, or a text. As Howard Becker argues, these patrons could choose freely to support whomever they deemed worthy, regardless of the artist's or maker's reputation. However, throughout the history of art worlds, generous patrons were often the sole means by which artists could sustain themselves, continue creating, and eventually gain widespread recognition. Another critical observation by the sociologist concerns the concept of "government patronage",[54] which may vary across political regimes. This point is particularly significant in this current historical moment marked by increasing cuts to arts and

52. The Salon des Refusēs (1863) was an exhibition organized by Napoleon III to showcase works rejected by the official Paris Salon.
53. Howard Becker, *Art Worlds* (University of California Press, 1982), 113.
54. Becker, *Art Worlds*, 107.

humanities funding, driven by the growing dominance of right-wing politics and their agendas. As suggested by the sociologist: "When the government sees artistic activities as supporting national interests, it provides financial support which otherwise would have to come from elsewhere or would not be available at all. It may give a direct financial subsidy, to be spent as the individual artist or the organizers of the art group see fit; or access to government-owned exhibition or performance spaces which otherwise would have to be paid for; or materials or salaries for specific personnel or categories of personnel."[55] But what then happens when practices are not state-funded anymore?

In our modern era, the concept of patronage has evolved and is now closely associated with platforms, with one main pioneer of this model even bearing a nearly identical name: *Patreon*.[56] In the digital age, artists and thinkers, regardless of their field, can connect with their audiences online and attract supporters willing to subscribe to and sustain their work. In this context, the patron is no longer a wealthy individual but rather someone who recognizes value in an individual's practice and chooses to contribute a modest monthly fee. This model aligns with the idea that, for any creator to sustain their work, they need only find a thousand people willing to support them consistently each month. While reaching such a number might seem challenging, many argue that it is far from impossible. This strategy of micro-funding is one that also has been applied to media companies to remain independent and develop stories or opinionated pieces that

55. Becker, *Art Worlds*, 182.
56. *Patreon* is a platform that allows creators to earn recurring revenue from their supporters, known as "patrons." It enables creators—such as artists, musicians, writers, podcasters, and other content creators—to offer exclusive content, experiences, or rewards in exchange for financial support.

could be critical no matter what, such as *Mediapart*.[57] Yet, is the economy of independence and self-organized thinkers a realistic and attainable utopia?

In *Entreprecariat,* Silvio Russo draws a genealogy of Silicon Valley and its myths, which, as he argues, sculpted the definition of entrepreneurship today. [58] As discussed by the author, the concept of precarity for the entrepreneur is embedded within two opposing notions of freedom and subjugation. As entrepreneurs operate within the constraints of capitalist maneuvers, they often move away from most of their social rights.[59] In an effort to become self-employed, entrepreneurs must actively position themselves within the market with a unique and original offering, seeing themselves not only as a necessity but also as a highly disciplined individual who, through the turnover of their agenda, can make their universe thrive. As illustrated in Silvio Russo's book, in this endless quest to self-realize, the entrepreneur falls into a devotion that the designer and writer calls "an ill-considered self-help exercise."[60] However, taking the risk of becoming a freelancer on the margins of institutions requires a certain amount of privilege. In the article "There's No Way That You Get Paid to Do the Arts: Unpaid Labour Across the Cultural and Creative Life Course", Orian Brook and Dave O'Brien dissected the terminologies and criteria that can help one assess the links between unpaid work and precariousness. Under prevailing conditions, individuals only can partake in low levels of non-wage benefits (holidays or sickness pay, financial security), etc. They further argue how such

57. *Mediapart* is an independent French online investigative journal, founded in 2008 by Edwy Plenel and others, known for its in–depth reporting, editorial independence, and subscription–based model that eschews advertising.
58. Silvio Lorusso, *Entreprecariat* (Onomatopee, 2019), 22.
59. Lorusso, *Entreprecariat*, 41.
60. Lorusso, *Entreprecariat*, 68

a positioning can only be tolerated or enrolled by "those with more resources", as they "are more able to afford unpaid work."[61] Circling back to critical internet research, it is essential to ensure that such practices are not exclusively sustained by white privilege and individuals from already highly educated households, such that techno-criticism may accommodate and consider diverse perspectives to the benefit of everyone, as a matter of principle and practice.

Aware of the limitations and exclusions endemic to a system centered on the self as an institution or commodity, our economy thrives on sustaining this type of business model as an ideal. But what makes it so alluring overall - beyond the pursuit of personal brands for the dispersal of content? Are we being sold an artificially new dream of theory and research-making, and this way truly the only alternative? The book *The Dark Forest Theory of the Internet* not only encourages digital creators and online thinkers to venture off the beaten path, it also introduces a critique of the concept of the individual and its many enterprises, as well as an invitation to rethink what is at stake when we collectively aim for in a post-individualist world. In his essay, *The Post Individual,* Yancey Strickler, founder of the start-up and successful crowd-funding platform Kickstarter, displays how our need to self-actualize through consumerism and various medals or forms of self-recognition might be about to collapse.[62] In such an era of shift and movement, *The Dark Forest* aims to illustrate all the online gatherings that are said to be "unindexed, non-optimized, non-gamified, and hidden from

61. Orian Brook, Dave O' Brien, and Mark Taylor, "'There's No Way That You Get Paid to Do the Arts': Unpaid Labour Across the Cultural and Creative Life Course," *Sociological Research Online* 25, no. 4 (December 1, 2020): 571-88, https://doi.org/10.1177/1360780419895291.
62. Jay David Bolter, *The Digital Plenitude: The Decline of Elite Culture and the Rise of New Media* (The MIT Press, 2019), 172.

public view", where researchers and creators can come and create networks that hold the potential to become more sustainable than those hosted on commercial platforms, with their dependencies and pitfalls.[63] All in all, not too far from the vision of Geert Lovink in his book *Dark Fiber*. To prioritize community over individualism, virtual intellectuals must establish their presence, produce content, and occasionally perform to cultivate audiences and gain recognition.

63.   Bolter, *The Digital Plenitude*, 197.

The Virtual Intellectual and the Commodification of Knowledge Online

Returning to *Digital Plenitude*, where Jay David Bolter explored the evolution of media and communication into distinct mediums and disciplines into a central element of our daily lives and consumption, the theorist underlines how: "this loss of the center, is not a "problem" to be solved. It is simply the condition of our culture today."[64] In comparing the two eras, Jay David Bolter invites us to consider the once-assumed hierarchy between high culture and mass culture, a distinction that has largely dissolved in the present day, primarily due to the internet and the swift proliferation of knowledge creation and dissemination online. But for Jay David Bolter, it is not only a merging of culture and class but rather, the notion of distinction that seems to have lost its legitimacy, to the point where, for many people, "art and media are now the same things."[65] For context, the writer reminds us that this happens to be particularly true in nations where there exists a low level of public support for the traditional arts, such as the United States. He emphasizes how: "the situation in Europe is more ambiguous, and in general the distinction between high culture and popular culture has faded more slowly there."[66]

---

64. Jay David Bolter, *The Digital Plenitude: The Decline of Elite Culture and the Rise of New Media* (The MIT Press, 2019), 2.
65. Bolter, *The Digital Plenitude*, 15.
66. Bolter, *The Digital Plenitude*, 16.

In this framework, the virtual intellectual embodies a phenomenon highlighted by Jay David Bolter, functioning both as a product of this shift and as a catalyst for cultivating an appreciation of media culture as a thoughtful and respectful medium for generating and engaging with theory. But whether we examine Joshua Citarella or other creators involved in critical internet research in the era of *Digital Plenitude*, we also consequently witness the commodification of knowledge online. Commodification, as such, echoes privatization, as it refers to "the fact that something is treated or considered as a commodity (= a product that can be bought and sold.)"[67] These days, the commodification of research might appear more prominent and evident on social media in the form of YouTube essays containing product recommendations or philosophical essays restricted behind paywalls - a shift that can feel challenging for traditionalists.[68] Indeed, such individuals may struggle to reconcile with how far the privatization and commercialization of knowledge have progressed; they may question the trajectory of this digital plenitude, deranged by the phenomenon that media and philosophy are now mass consumed through YouTube essays with sponsored ads or published on micro-subsidized online portals. However, were institutions and knowledge-production systems ever truly free and accessible to all? At certain points in history, and in specific parts of the world, universities and access to knowledge were publicly funded or offered for free, supported by state resources. However, this ideal has never been universally achieved and is now in decline, exacerbating disparities in the accessibility of traditional houses of knowledge across regions and systems.

---

67. "Commodification," in *Cambridge Dictionnary*, accessed December 12, 2024, https://dictionary.cambridge.org/dictionary/english/commodification.
68. Bolter, *The Digital Plenitude*, 165.

In the article *The Commodification of Academic Research: Science and the Modern University,* Hans Rader reminds us that commercial profit isn't something that is only being pursued in the commercial and corporate world: "commodification is identified with commercialization, that is, the pursuit of profit by academic institutions through selling the expertise of their researchers and the results of their inquiries."[69] As commodification became evident across various industries, researchers employed by academic institutions began to run their businesses as well after recognizing the growing demand for their expertise, whether for consulting, corporate work, or content creation.[70] Any criticism scrutinizing the commodification of online research as merely a tool for capitalist exploitation becomes less convincing in a context where academic structures themselves perpetuate dynamics that are marginally different from, yet fundamentally similar to, those of a business model. However, it was not solely the sudden awareness of academia's inherent limitations and flaws that led thinkers and artists to distance themselves from it. Rather, this shift reflected a broader cultural transformation in the production of knowledge, encompassing its hierarchies, structures, and meaning.[71]

The results of such fragmentations, which have enabled and accelerated the explosion of new cultures, are mentioned by Jay David Bolter, who underlines the potential for a radical democratization of culture. However, such phenomena and trends must not only be produced and analyzed; they must also be scrutinized and dissected, a job that critical internet research, for example, often manages to organize and produce on time. And still, Bolter

69. Hans Radder, ed., *The Commodification of Academic Research* (University of Pittsburgh Press, 2010), 4.
70. Radder, *The Commodification of Academic Research,* 8.
71. Jay David Bolter, *The Digital Plenitude: The Decline of Elite Culture and the Rise of New Media* (The MIT Press, 2019), 51.

argues that even amidst such plenitude, not everyone participating is capable of judging and reflecting upon the novel subcultures and trends they are partaking in and developing: "This creativity may be blandly appreciated as universal, but it can only be evaluated about one or more of the appropriate communities. There is no single standard, and no community's creative practice is central to all of our culture."[72] The notion of such a disruption of culture and knowledge-making, which has been regarded by theorists as a "cultural disaster",[73] is a view located on the other side of the spectrum. For many digital enthusiasts, the same phenomenon is considered a liberation, especially for all of those who did not have a platform previously. This clash seriously demonstrates the reluctance of a certain elite class to surrender their power and their hegemony to a more mainstream audience and generative ecosystem. As Jay David Bolter argues, those who long for the nostalgia of traditional standards are clinging to the outdated ways and structures of a bygone era, now fragmented and dismantled. After all, "diversity in entertainment, art, and cultural expression should not be a cause for concern."[74]

The popularization of research, critical thinking, and analysis would be widely celebrated and embraced in a world where digital platforms already could rely on a proven track record of doing more good than harm if they were properly regulated. As previously noted, the quality and authenticity of online content can easily be called into question and is sometimes analyzed too hastily. As time goes by, the internet may become less and less of a reliable source for information, instead pooling random topics and AI-generated fake news or disinformation. In one of his latest books, *Internet Extinction,* Geert Lovink

74. Bolter, *The Digital Plenitude,* 189.

elaborates on this notion, inviting the reader to question the current state of the art of the internet as it is: "We know the state of disorder in the context of internet critique as the problem of information overload with its mental symptoms of distraction, exhaustion, and anxiety, precipitated by subliminal extractivist social media architectures",[75] inviting the reader to rethink the possible strategies and tools to formulate a radical critique of our current networks. In this context, researchers will need a very different strategy, one that goes beyond the digitization of archives with good-looking graphics, and rather focuses on investigative aesthetics and their relation to power structures.[76] But there's no more time for nostalgia, no more time for the disappearance of the "becoming internet": Geert Lovink insists on ways to properly destroy the internet as it is before the internet destroys itself. While it may seem too late to revive an internet that aligns with our collective ideals, hope is not lost. Alternative platforms are emerging at the minute when existing ones face criticism from virtual intellectuals. In this era, Geert Lovink emphasizes the importance of focusing on techno-social dynamics, shifting attention from platforms to protocols to better analyze and contemplate the future of technology.

An additional unintended consequence of the democratization of knowledge, though not the central focus of this research, warrants attention: the potential proliferation of pseudo-science and pseudo-intellectualism in online spaces. While this phenomenon might apply to many other disciplines than internet research or media studies, the overall fear is to see public and online figures using vetted and reliable references to build an argument that

75. Geert Lovink, *Extinction Internet* (Institute of Network Cultures, 2022), 14.
76. Lovink, *Extinction Internet*, 26.

favors their rhetoric without any proper analysis. In the YouTube video *No one wants to go to college anymore*, Alice Cappelle, a young French YouTuber doing cultural analysis emphasizes how her academic path led her to join YouTube, explaining how, in her view, academic research did not lead to potential employment: "It annoys me that most of the problem that I had with academia was to... start my channel, start my own business."[77] While her own experience within higher education and the success of her videos led her to change course, the YouTuber illustrates how this shift—from the hegemony of universities to their criticism, and now even their near downfall—could have disastrous consequences for the future of education and critical thinking. This concern is also explored by YouTube essayist Kidology in her video *Why We Can't Read Full Books Anymore.*[78]

77. *No One Wants to Go to College Anymore*, Youtube Video, 2024, https://www.youtube.com/watch?v=QzzRsgg5Ccc.
78. *Why We Can' t Read Full Books Anymore*, Youtube Video, 2024, https://www.youtube.com/watch?v=7fz–W–jVT1s&t=2279s.

The Self—Sustained Internet Thinker
After the Institutional Withdraw

While the criticism around intellectuals and their ideo-
logically driven self-employment is valid, it is easy to see
how this model has smoothly grown and integrated within
the context of the United States of America, where wel-
fare, education, and public funding for the arts and critical
practices at large are challenging to sustain and access,
often leaving only the most resourceful "hustlers" thriving. Referring to Joshua Citarella's post, abandoning traditional art education in favor of pursuing a career as an
influencer doesn't seem surprising—or even necessarily a
bad idea—in this context. For professional academics, offering classes for an affordable monthly fee, rather than
teaching at prohibitively expensive universities, could ar-
guably be seen as a form of activism against the privatization and costs of American universities. But can anyone
truly become a self-made virtual intellectual, and what
does it take to attempt to build an alternative institution?

    In *Can the Subscription-Based Model of the Music
Industry Fix the Art World?*, Loney Abrams pondered as
early as 2018 how the art world, like many other industries,
appeared in need of reform and questioned the viability of
economic models for creatives. The subscription economy, which, according to the journalist, was highly inspired
by the models experimented with and later implemented in
the music industry, rewards creators on a competitive and

more equitable revenue model: "The size of their fan base determines how much money they make."[79] The journalist ponders how visual artists could also benefit from such a system, hoping perhaps to get a better reward than mere visibility or access to the public via institutions. Further along in the article, the journalist presented the practice of Joshua Citarella, who, already in 2018, had started to experiment with such models by posting on his Drip account: "For $5 per month, 25 current subscribers receive a digital copy of a book Citarella produced, plus "behind the scenes content"; for $15 per month, five current subscribers receive a physical copy of the book; for $100 per month, three current subscribers (this tier caps at three subscribers) receive a unique 20-inch-by-16-inch artwork at the year's end."[80]

But of course, Joshua Citarella wasn't the first or the only one to use such a strategy as a way to sustain his means. Loney Abrams also mentioned Lauren Boyle, a member of the art collective DIS, a collective which had been busy since the 2010s producing videos and content about online cultures and their aesthetics. To sustain the platform and publish videos with a unique vision or aesthetics that didn't quite fit within the typical YouTube format or indie film scene, the collective DIS.Art also experimented with subscription-based models that provided access to archived videos and educational syllabi. Returning to *Art Worlds* by Howard Becker, we find ourselves far removed from the old patronage system, where a certain level of social capital was required to fund an

79. Loney Abrams, "New Artist Strategies, Pt. 1: Can the Subscription—Based Model of the Music Industry Fix the Art World?," Art Space, October 27, 2018, https://www.artspace.com/magazine/interviews_features/in_depth/new—artist—strategies—part—1—what—can—the—art—world—learn—from—the—subscription—based—model—of—the—55720.
80. Abrams, "New Artist Strategies, Pt. 1", 2018.

artist one admired or wished to see succeed. In this new subscription economy, individuals could pay a fee that is minor to the cost of a monthly visit to the museum, and enjoy regular access to content and news from their favorite creatives. However, as suggested by Howard Becker, within the more recent lineage of patronage, the psychology and success of the more recent monthly subscription or Patreon model is very much influenced by the reputation of the artist or platform in the first place. If one wants to find success on Patreon, one should better get known.

In *I Pick My Poison: Agency and Addiction in the Age of Subscriptions*, researchers Iveta Hajdakov and Morgan Williams study subscription model economies and different approaches to the concept of willingness-to-pay. Through their analysis, they demonstrate that this model of content accessibility, which is now adopted by most mainstream platforms (Netflix, YouTube, Amazon, etc.), altered consumer psychology over the years. Referring to the book *Subscribed,* where Tien Tzuo explained that the subscription economy represents a transformation in the way business is transacted, Iveta Hajakov and Morgan Williams formulate the defining characteristic of the subscription economy, which they claim to be a shift from a "product-centric business model to a customer-centric business model."[81] As a result of this transformation, they argue, "a new type of consumer emerges, one who pre-orders access to services or to the ownership of products. To cater to this new consumer, businesses need to leverage new tools, build new knowledge about their customers, and sustain the process and development of a customer relationship over time."[82] Although the duo's

81. Iveta Hajdakov and Morgan Williams, "I Pick My Poison": Agency and Addiction in the Age of Subscriptions" (Stripe Partners, 2024), 6.

82. Hajdakov and Williams, "I Pick My Poison", 8.

research is mostly applied to the relationship between users and big corporations, it is relevant to think of their analysis and reconsider it within the framework of the singular content creator as the main provider of such services.

In such an economy, the freelancer who delivers monthly content has to compete with other content creators and bigger companies that also provide subscription services. As a result, individual creators must constantly evaluate the quality of their work, often pushing their productivity to their limit. The rivalry is intense, as they face intense competition from larger platforms, which, backed by millions of monthly subscribers, can afford to offer high-end products and novelty in their services. In this battlefield, if patrons or subscribers recognize this distinction, their willingness to pay may vary between supporting an individual creator and subscribing to a large platform. The drivers for supporting an individual creator often stem from feelings of sympathy and appreciation for the effort they put into their work, and may also be influenced by para-social dynamics—the sense of a personal connection to the content creator. This is, perhaps, one of the most significant differences between the entrepreneur as a content creator and more prominent companies: the creator has to remain accessible, relatable, and engaged, while bigger corporations operate as neutral entities that do not need to provide a sense of personal connection or authenticity.

These US-centric strategies the willing-to-pay model, and other self-made ideologies have never been something Europe seemed eager to embrace. Interestingly, Joshua's decision to leave teaching and establish a researcher-influencer business model in 2019 has since been replicated across various fields and contexts. What was initially considered a controversial move, self-focused business strategy now appears to have become a necessary practice especially as funding and public support continue to dwindle.[83] As previously argued, while it is difficult to predict the exact measures right-wing governments might take regarding funding cuts, it is undeniable that many spaces—whether in the arts or research specifically—are facing severe budget reductions. To envision a framework that transcends the binary between the individualist business model and the abstract ideal of communism, it seems reasonable to explore the many ways to sustain research and experimentation beyond the diminishing means of institutional and state-funded support. It is relevant to note that, in some instances, even when researchers could benefit from academic or institutional support, they deliberately chose to forge a parallel path. Indeed, Joshua Citarella is not the only figure focused on internet culture and contemporary society who, despite an impressive CV and background, has chosen to step back from traditional academic paths. Figures like Kideology, Contrapoints, Alice Cappelle, and Internet Analysis have similar backgrounds in the humanities and social sciences, yet they have opted to pursue careers in social media instead.

While their reasons may not always be explicitly stated, common themes include the lack of job security, intense competition, and an elitist atmosphere within academia,[84] factors that conflict with their personal goals and, perhaps, with the needs of their audiences. Despite the numerous arguments as to why such figures have moved away from academic careers to primarily publish

83. Senay Boztas, "'Culture Is Fragile': Dutch Art World Figures Express Concerns for Future under Potential Coalition Government," *The Art Newspaper*, January 19, 2024, https://www.theartnewspaper.com/2024/01/19/culture-is-fragile-dutch-art-world-figures-express-concerns-for-future-under-potential-coalition-government.
84. *No One Wants to Go to College Anymore*, Youtube Video, 2024, https://www.youtube.com/watch?v=QzzRsgg5Ccc.

their research and findings online, it is important to note, however, that the individuals discussed in this text are highly educated, often holding an MA or even a PhD. As such, it would be naive and reductive to claim that such figures did not benefit from the structured learning and methodologies provided during their academic studies. And still, within the specific context of digital cultures and internet theory, such a withdrawal seems to also align somewhat with the argument that its nature and objects do not always fit the strict requirements of analysis within academia,[85] leading highly capable and educated researchers and thinkers to draw their path, sharing and experimenting with their research on other platforms. Yet, there exists a complexity around the timeline of analysis when it is done outside of academia's standards: the rapid evolution of the web and its most advanced developments often outpace the speed at which analysis and criticism can respond.

85. As quoted in the interview with Geert Lovink.

INTERNET
THEORY ON THE
PLATFORM

Theory with Influencer Stylings

As previously introduced, there exist many different models and strategies for becoming an independent online researcher that offer alternatives to traditional institutional ties. Successful YouTube channels and podcasts delivering and rendering research demonstrate that individuals don't always need to show their faces to be known, recognized, and valued. However, establishing an identity and developing a consistent branding strategy—as with many other forms of empire-building—remains a crucial component for the virtual intellectual.[86] For content creators, crafting a website, selecting fonts and colors, maintaining a regular publishing schedule, and incorporating elements of storytelling are all vital. In this new space driven more heavily by narrative, the use of the self—one's voice, face, and opinions—long rejected by traditional academic standards of rigor, has proven highly effective. This personal and customizable approach fosters meaningful connections between audiences and content creators, ensuring sustained engagement and conversations over time.

What is particularly fascinating about the figure of the internet critical researcher as they present themselves online, is that the visual delivery of their research often mirrors the content they're dissecting: their aesthetics often align with the norms and standards of online spaces.

86. Geert Lovink, "Portrait of the Virtual Intellectual," Nettime (blog), July 20, 1997, nettime.

In this process, the researcher not only has to produce the content they aim to analyze or critique but must also master the rules and strategies of editing, posting, and optimizing—just like any other content creator would. There again, Joshua Citarella serves as an intriguing case study, as he explored the subcultures of Looksmaxxing while simultaneously undergoing his physical transformation through a highly specific diet and an intense gym routine.[87] Currently, his Patreon offers a range of media and content for a reasonable fee, including a curated monthly reading list, exclusive podcast access, and a personalized workout routine. An archived talk of Geert Lovink on the topic of the virtual intellectual, available on net.time, refers to Eduard Said, who, "insisted that the intellectual is "an individual with a specific public role in society that cannot be reduced to being a faceless professional."[88] Not only does the virtual or intellectual influencer have to be present online and offline, using digitized and non-digitized source material, but he also, as argued by Geert Lovink, has to challenge the presentation of their work beyond text: "Since s/he has been educated in the heritage of the text, the virtual intellectual now will be confronted by the problem of the visualization of ideas. Text-only systems can no longer be auto-poetic."[89] This is a gesture that Joshua Citarella and other critical internet researchers are actively attempting to execute and orchestrate over time.

Adopting the strategies of influencers to promote critical thinking or disseminate various theories might initially seem unconventional, perhaps even problematic. After

87. Joshua Citarella, "Auto—Experiment: Hyper—Masculinity," subscription—based platform, *Patreon* (blog), September 8, 2021, https://www.patreon.com/posts/auto—experiment-55888347.
88. Edward W. Said, *Representations of the Intellectual* (Vintage, 1996), 83.
89. Geert Lovink, "Portrait of the Virtual Intellectual," *Nettime* (blog), July 20, 1997, nettime.

all, isn't being an influencer primarily about sharing pleasant daily routines and entertainment, which has historically been constructed as opposite to critical thinking? In the introduction of the book *The Influencer Factory A Marxist Theory of Corporate Personhood on YouTube* Grant Bollmer and Katherine Guinness start their investigation by stating the unavoidable: "Influencers are an integral category for the reproduction of the social relation that is capitalism."[90] In the process of exploiting the self as a commodity, the persona has a brand, which eventually, if sustainable, has to turn into a business, and invites all creators and consumers to rethink what sharing and community can mean online. In this totalizing, dream-like space, where creators entice everyone else to quit the rat race and join them in commodifying the self to become unalienated: "only through complete alienation, in which the last product one fabricates is one's own identity and body, can one transcend alienation."[91] Behind the narratives of content creators lie numerous fantasies and illusions: the promise of fulfillment through self-production and promotion, the allure of community, and the ideal of resource sharing. However, these tales often overlook the reality that this labor relies heavily on performativity, which frequently leads to burnout and exhaustion as individuals attempt to extract and monetize their very sense of self.[92]

While literature on influencer culture is still limited, books and guides on how to use social media effectively are thriving online. Numerous titles, including Get Rich or Lie Trying by Symeon Brown, explore the myriad ways to navigate platforms, highlighting the clever strategies of figures like Soulja Boy, the music scammer, all while

90. Grant Bollmer and Katherine Guinness, *The Influencer Factory: A Marxist Theory of Corporate Personhood on YouTube* (Standorf University Press, 2024), 4.
91. Bollmer, *The Influencer Factory*, 38.
92. Bollmer, *The Influencer Factory*, 41.

emphasizing: "All this can be yours...if you're willing to do it right."[93] While the subject of such books tends to be influencer models in general rather than the specific concept and figure of the virtual intellectual, they remain insightful, offering a glimpse into the existing pipelines of content creation and business model development currently thriving online.[94] Celebrities, authorities, experts... the market for influencer strategy holds a niche for everyone, so the guru says. What you will do doesn't matter as much as the plan you have in mind. "What is your endgame?" Symeon Brown asks, prompting the reader to think two, three, perhaps even four years ahead of time to better understand how to build a strategy.[95] Objective setting is where the fun begins, or so says the book, quoting Pablo Picasso and other successful artists. Although these books may seem like scam material to many, they cover the fundamentals of marketing and public relations, introducing readers to the tools anyone looking to grow a business should consider. As such, Symeon Brown does not sell us dreams. On the contrary, he emphasizes how the business of influence online comprises much more than taking simple videos and shots and publishing them on social media: these are business plans and objectives, requiring strategic collaboration with the right partners, as well as long-term alliances.

Beyond the business plan, influencers may make use of many further frameworks and concepts to better define their prospects. Even a strategically placed imperfection could work wonders to remain attractive in the eyes of the viewers and followers. Once the business goals and dreams are designed, now comes the hardest part: finding and reaching your audience.[96] For influencers and virtual intellectuals alike, the idea and projection of authenticity and relatability are

93. Symeon Brown, *Get Rich or Lie Trying* (Atlantic Books, 2023), 4.
94. Brown, *Get Rich or Lie Trying*, 33.
95. Brown, *Get Rich or Lie Trying*, 72.

crucial As previously mentioned, an influencer must do more than, simply share facts and sources; the subjects of study must also be presented in a visually engaging and contextually appropriate manner. Consequently, thinkers and theorists aiming to share their research online must carefully examine the relevant content, niche, and aesthetics they can leverage, given the competitive and demanding nature of the digital marketplace. Influential creators, such as ContraPoints, Philosophy Tube, and Joshua Citarella, demonstrate the power of storytelling and cinematic techniques in crafting knowledge-rich, compelling content. Such videos may take weeks or even months to produce and edit, but the effort appears to be justified. In the end, what matters is the quality of the work, its aesthetic appeal, and its ability to captivate audiences in an attention economy where focus and attention are scarce.

96. Brown, *Get Rich or Lie Trying*, 20.

Theory and Research at the Pace of the Attention Economy

As early as 1971, Simon Hebert raised the question in *Designing Organizations for an Information-rich World* about the consequences of attention scarcity in an information-overloaded world. In his research, he tackled the design problem of organizations to make them operate efficiently regarding the allocation of scarce attention: "In an information-rich world, the wealth of information means a death of something else: a scarcity of whatever it is that information consumes. What information consumes is rather obvious: it consumes the attention of its recipients. Hence a wealth of information creates a poverty of attention and a need to allocate that attention efficiently among the overabundance of information sources that might consume it."[97] In this landscape, virtual intellectuals don't produce mind-blowing and technically challenging work solely for its aesthetic value; they also do so out of necessity. Scrolling through endless videos of cat memes and vegan recipes, audiences are now well-educated and informed about the myriad of possibilities that scrolling offers them. It is well-known and acknowledged that information overload leads to widespread loss and waste of time. As a matter of fact, the audience might as well have a good, or silly time, if only to forget about the moment that fled away.

97. Simon Hebert, *Designing Organizations for an Information–Rich World*, vol. Computers, Communications, and the Public Interest. (Johns Hopkins Press, 1971), 40–41.

In the book *Stand Out of Our Light. Freedom and Resistance in the Attention Economy*, James Williams dissects the condition and the possibilities at hand in what has become the biggest vacuum of intentionality of the 21st century: "What do you pay when you pay attention? You pay with all the things you could have attended to, but didn't: all the goals you didn't pursue, all the actions you didn't take, and all the possible things you could have been, had you attended to those other things. Attention is paid to possible futures foregone."[98] As such, it can feel both unsettling and contradictory to consider participating in the attention economy, specifically when it comes to sharing resources, knowledge, politics, or activism. Why participate in the race for the most click-worthy, superficial, yet exciting methods of content creation? After all, isn't research meant to stand in contrast to such fast-paced and poorly rendered conditions? As previously introduced, the common defense of academic and scientific knowledge production is that it allows for a slower, more deliberate, and profound approach and that peer-to-peer analysis is essential for ensuring that knowledge is produced and processed, even amidst the rapid and turbulent pace of modern society and news cycles. But this timely pressure is now felt everywhere. The urgency and stress of the race for the attention economy are also felt by journals, media outlets, and platforms, which must constantly produce more content and break news faster than TikTokers or content creators surrounded by flashy teams that help to generate a constant shimmer and energy around the material.

And still, an intriguing challenge emerges in the realm of internet studies and digital culture. If the role of thinkers, critical creators, and journalists is to inform and educate the public on technological developments and their

98. James Williams, *Stand out of Our Light* (Cambridge University Press, 2018), 35.

impact, they must think quickly, as techno-capitalism moves at a pace far faster than the state can process or lawyers can anticipate. However, the goal here is not to rush and produce critical thinking in response to every new trend or ideology, but rather to think alongside the internet and digital evolution, to retain an awareness of the youth and their interests, and to explore the best ways to involve more individuals in this ongoing debate. But once one understands the pressures and obligations imposed by platforms—pressures that apply to all creators—it becomes natural to question the quality and authenticity of the content being produced. In an economy where attention and algorithmic decision-making dominate, replacing the patience to analyze and evaluate, the attempt to produce and share theory at a pace aligned with human capacity seems vain and futile. On these platforms, established creators and scientists who can afford to publish on social media with accuracy and technical expertise rarely work alone; behind them is often a small team supporting their efforts, replicating structural and organizational dynamics. So, how can one compete?

Another contentious aspect of critical internet research produced online relates to the ideology of democratic and public knowledge: research should remain independent and free from specific conflicts of interest,[99] particularly financial ones, and should never be prone to paid sponsorships. As such, choosing topics of research and analysis based on their plausible popularity has been questioned and criticized. However, it also seems evident that if virtual intellectuals need to sustain themselves,

99. "Disclosure of Interests and Management of Conflicts of Interest," edu, University of Queensland (blog), accessed December 22, 2024, https://research-support.uq.edu.au/resources-and-support/ethics-integrity-and-compliance/research-integrity/disclosure-interests-and-management-conflicts-interest.

they will inevitably consider what aligns with their best economic interests and perhaps shift their content and direction towards what works best online. To suggest that the practice of internet researchers or virtual intellectuals can exist without being influenced by economic and strategic decision-making would be illusory and perpetuate the notion that anyone can simply conduct research in their free time.[100] A tale that is not only false but also reinforces the elitist framework that determines who can produce knowledge and who cannot.

100. Orian Brook, Dave O' Brien, and Mark Taylor, "'There's No Way That You Get Paid to Do the Arts': Unpaid Labour Across the Cultural and Creative Life Course," Sociological Research Online 25, no. 4 (December 1, 2020): 571-88, https://doi.org/10.1177/1360780419895291.

The Critique of
Critical Internet Research

As introduced earlier, a common critique of critical internet research—outside the scope of academic papers or peer-reviewed journals—is that it often leans more on personal opinions than on well-structured, research-driven insights.[101] When posted to blogs, YouTube videos, or podcasts, the practice of sharing insights and criticism without rigorous methods or expertise to back them up frequently leads to discussions about the oversimplification of certain subjects. These critiques are increasingly prominent in the U.S., where individuals, often for financial reasons, may be more likely to choose not to pursue university education.[102] But how can we proceed when the content produced and explored through academic research fails to reach a broader public audience outside of its own specific academic bubble? How can we ensure that internet and digital criticism reaches a wider public of internet users, who could benefit from a critical perspective on the development of technology and platforms, encouraging reflection on what is being produced and how? If it is not intended to educate its this audience, then who is it for? Joshua Citarella

---

101. Jeremy Hunsinger, Matthew M.Allen, and Lisbeth Klastrup, eds., *Second International Handbook of Internet Research* (Springer, 2020), 398.
102. Roisin Lanigan, "Nobody Wants to Go to College Anymore," I-D, November 2, 2021, https://i-d.co/article/college-admissions-university-decrease/.

and Geert Lovink share a similar approach to publishing internet theory: whether through the Institute of Network Cultures or Do Not Research; they avoid academic rigidity and strict boundaries. Instead, they prioritize empirical research and experimental formats that showcase diverse and inclusive applications of critical thinking. However, this does not imply that any text can be published on their platforms. A closer examination of research published on *Do Not Research* or the Institute of Network Culture reveals that each piece, although speculative or experimental, is well-referenced and articulated.

Returning to critical insight on the pace of content production and its potential superficiality, the speed at which critical internet research is shared, discussed, and produced is undeniably faster than what academic rigor would traditionally permit. However, the question of knowledge production should not be about who is the fastest and most productive, as this would replicate the structural issues inherent to the academic publishing model. Instead, the underlying argument is the following: in the context of internet culture and theory, a certain agility and pace must be tolerated due to the fragile and fast-changing nature of these subjects. This isn't a call to abolish digital culture and media departments, which provide a grounded, slower-paced approach that enables more precise and regulated critique. Relying solely on these institutions to understand our rapidly evolving world is both naive and outdated. This perspective is also explored in the book *Academia versus the World Outside*, where Bruce Fleming critiques the accumulated limitations and frustrations within the humanities and social sciences. The writer argues that the rigorous methods borrowed from science and the emphasis on constructing arguments about an "objective" world are both reductive and limiting.[103]

103. Bruce Fleming, *Academia versus the World Outside* (190: Routledge, 2024), 4.

While his argument applies to more than one field of discipline, Bruce Fleming illustrates the discontent felt by researchers and students who lack a sense of connection between the criticism formed in academia and the real world,[104] a frustration that appears to resolve when researchers apply more experimental and less rigorous methods of analysis.[105]

Nevertheless, it is essential to recognize that the proliferation of fake news and the presence of bots increasingly threaten the pursuit of rigorous internet study and critique. This issue can, for example, be examined through the lens of the "Dead Internet Theory", or the belief that everything on the internet is fake or generated by AI.[106] Indeed, such conspiracy theories drive researchers to raise a critical question: why bother engaging in critique when so much of the content it would sit next to lacks authenticity? The increased proliferation of AI-generated fake content diminishes trust and erodes the motivation to question or critique what is seen online. In this context, reliable sources like books and scientific papers become crucial pillars for grounding our understanding, highlighting the need for robust structures of credibility.[107] As the internet continues to be inundated with fake and misleading content, how can we effectively critique or create a digital space that is changing so rapidly? We are presented with the find ways to preserve meaningful critical discourse online.

Finally, a significant complexity lies in the discourse around knowledge-making and its fundamental accessibility. As previously emphasized, none of the thinkers or

104. Fleming, *Academia versus the World Outside*, 35.
105. Fleming, *Academia versus the World Outside*, 56.
106. Illuminati Pirate, "Dead Internet Theory: Most of the Internet Is Fake," Forum, *Agoraroad*, January 5, 2021, https://forum.agoraroad.com/index.php?threads/dead-internet-theory-most-of-the-internet-is-fake.3011/.
107. Richard Rogers, *Digital Methods* (The MIT Press, 2013), 31.

creators mentioned can be considered self-made in the sense of having entirely bypassed academia or formal institutions. As such, it would be misleading and insincere to argue that critical thinking can develop entirely outside the box, as the necessary fundamental understanding often requires familiarity with the box's boundaries. Thinkers like Geert Lovink, and Joshua Citarella, and YouTubers like Kidology or Alice Cappelle have benefited from high-quality university education. Thus, the argument shifts—not to a fundamental critique of academia itself, but rather to a critique of how its principles are applied in other fields where research needs to be more speculative and rapidly produced to remain relevant within its discourse. Acknowledging all these possible critics, it would be naive too to assume that internet research fits neatly into only two or three distinct categories: one confined to academia, the other tailored for marketing purposes, and the last one being a superficial analysis of algorithmic pleasings. Whether conducted via Discord channels, in para-academic settings funded by philanthropic organizations or organized virtually through think tanks or simple email and newsletters, critical internet research follows many different pathways, applying any necessary strategies.

VIRTUAL INTELLECTUAL AND THE PROCESS OF ONLINE BECOMING

Becoming the Product

When critical internet researchers start producing content that is delivered and experienced online, they become "prosumers." This term, introduced by Alvin Toffler in his influential 1980 work *The Third Wave*, describes individuals who merge the roles of producer and consumer by creating goods and services either for their use or for communal sharing. While these terms might apply to more services and applications than to critical internet researchers, they appear to be relevant when thinking of knowledge production and the blurred divide between individual and milieu referred to by Jay David Bolter in *Digital Plenitude*. Indeed, social media and internet platforms allow individuals to access and integrate references and information into their daily lives. As a result, users or consumers may develop a perceived sense of expertise or familiarity with the practices and knowledge in the fields they engage with, and therefore start creating content or products too. However, in the specific context of critical internet research, as previously demonstrated, this production involves not only the creation of a product but also becoming a product oneself, as it requires individuals to embody, to some extent, the role of a virtual intellectual.

"Becoming the product",[108] as in, embodying the strategy of tailoring content or adopting Joshua Citarella's

108. Becoming the product is a concept I fabricated to better develop my argument in the following section.

aesthetic approach that parallels the content shared, can appear challenging, as it involves conforming to or performatively aligning with capitalist and manipulative tactics to deliver a particular message. However, given the current landscape in which news, media, and knowledge are produced, becoming the product implies a more nuanced molding and a critical awareness of what is at stake when attempting to present speculative and critical thinking online. While some content creators attribute their success to so-called "algorithmic magic",[109] a passive and not strategic approach rarely leads to meaningful engagement. To navigate algorithmic filters and gain visibility, content creators must study, analyze, and master the system. Success relies on adhering to the "rules of the game" and understanding what resonates and captures attention. By tailoring their content to align with these insights, creators maximize their chances of reaching their audience and achieving profitability. These strategies can vary widely, from performing a trending dance or using a popular sound to adopting a viral reel format or crafting an eye-catching headline. While these methods might appear trivial at first glance, they highlight the significant challenges these platforms face in the highly competitive attention economy, where content is constantly evolving to be shorter, more engaging, and increasingly irresistible. [110]

One of the many critical issues with such strategies is that they replicate the rules and rigidity imposed by the platforms themselves, compelling the intellectual, artist, or researcher to operate within these constraints, and sometimes limit their modes of action. As this alignment

109. Betti Marenko, "Algorithm Magic: Gilbert Simondon and Techno–Animism," in *Believing in Bits: Digital Media and the Supernatural,* ed. Simone Natale and Diana Pasulka (Oxford University Press, 2019).

110. "Subsight: Subverting the Attention Economy," 2022, https://subsight.netlify.app/theory/.

deepens, a dependency on the visibility and revenue generated by the platform naturally develops, creating a different, still similar dependency. If using the internet, social media, or click-bait strategies for visibility is often criticized, studies have shown that these approaches can yield positive outcomes, particularly in politics and activism and when representing marginalized groups.[111] In an age where both content and medium are the message, it would seem shortsighted not to leverage platforms that offer a chance to amplify one's voice. The strategy may appear superficial, even juvenile, yet the real is being revealed: when it comes to presenting theory, whether critical or speculative, is it insightful to avoid these platforms—or is it, rather, naive and idealistic to shun them altogether?

Within this quest, becoming the product aligns with the complex interplay of aesthetics and politics,[112] underscoring how messages, regardless of content, must adopt specific formats and visuals to gain visibility. In this context, Joshua Citarella serves as an intriguing example as his research transcends traditional mediums like papers or audio files, adapting instead to content structures that fit particular genres and aesthetics, illustrating the analysis of Jay David Bolter in *Digital Plenitude*. Although his delivery might appear mainstream, Joshua Citarella, for instance, consistently provides his audience with a mix of philosophical works, high literature, and even a fitness syllabus. In this context, gym rats can learn about media and internet theory, and digital nerds can learn about fitness

111. Chloe Arkenbout, "The Academic Value of Bottom—up Knowledge Produced by Marginalized Groups: The Relevance of Instagram Infographics for Ethical Terminology Frameworks," *Master of Media UVA, Webpage,* October 3, 2021, https://mastersofmedia.hum. uva.nl/2021/10/the—academic—value—of—bottom—up—knowledge— produced—by—marginalized—groups—the—relevance—of— instagram—infographics—for—ethical—terminology—frameworks/?.

112. Jacques Rancière, *History, Politics, Aesthetics* (Duke University Press Books, 2009), 2.

and nutrition. Whether this represents a performative aspect or a true blending of lifestyle and theory becomes irrelevant: once the researcher has entered the content creation and media pipeline they must continuously engage with and exist within it, a strategy that has also been analyzed through the figure of Slavoj Zizek in *How Slavoj Became Žižek: The Digital Making of a Public Intellectual* by Eliran Bar-El.

There remains, nevertheless, a dream of empowerment that transcends the application of copied strategies and surfaces to one's career and life. As they become the product, virtual intellectuals know that they are following a mainstream path, but they do so pragmatically in order to share their research and the products of their intellect widely. In itself, the mere desire for becoming the product isn't instrumental and often does not lead to the routes of fame and wealth. So, the product has to find ways to enjoy the long and steady process. However, one cannot merely become a product for the sake of itself: the product must carry a message or mission that reaches beyond the pursuit of economic outcomes and metrics.[113] Beyond the instrumentalisation of aesthetics to circulate knowledge or politics, "becoming the product" suggests that recognizing and exposing power structures for their superficiality can help individuals build new relationships towards imposed norms and mitigate criticism.

As such, "becoming the product" is a strategy that extends beyond content creation; it serves as a metaphor for any strategy needed to fit knowledge-making within molds of creation and perception. To assume that performativity and strategic positioning exist only within the pipelines of social media platforms would be ironic when considering the rigid rules and expectations pervading academia and

113. Silvio Lorusso, *Entreprecariat* (Onomatopee, 2019), 68.

the corporate world. Both realms also impose norms and stigmas that must be understood and enacted to succeed—or simply to stay relevant. They even often merge, too. Returning to *How Slavoj Became Žižek: The Digital Making of a Public Intellectual,* Eliran Bar-El writes: "With the rise of digital communication and new social media, today's technology intellectuals work in the attention economy. They succeed if they attract enough attention to themselves and their message that they can make a living from it."[114] But this attention sometimes functions as a trade-off, argues the researcher, as for it influencers may pay the price of "public suicide", coloring the image of the intellectual ridiculous or less serious.[115] One may argue that such suicide is worth the trade if it enables knowledge and criticism to reach broader audiences, enabling not only the democratization of knowledge but also its popularisation.[116] While this approach may not hold up to all critical perspectives, it can help shift our focus beyond mere content creation for views, justifying the strategic use of capitalist platforms and their extractive strategies for an extraneous and supposedly deeper, more virtuous purpose.

114. Eliran Bar–El, *How Slavoj Became Zizek* (Univeristy of Chicago Press, 2023), 7.
115. Bar–El, *How Slavoj Became Zizek,* 132.
116. Bar–El, *How Slavoj Became Zizek,* 177.

Theory Girl

Continuing with the concept of the virtual intellectual under the influence of platform incentives and algorithmic imperatives, it seems fitting to examine how gender performativity manifests in the delivery of content or research. So far, the primary figures discussed in this research are highly educated white men with substantial knowledge and access. While their achievements and efforts are undeniably significant, one cannot consider the effects of being a public figure or being an influencer without looking into the underlying gender performativity dynamics that can apply. Especially considering the patriarchal heritage of theory and its socio-cultural hierarchies. Assuming that everyone can produce knowledge and become a public figure without rendering the biases and preferences of audiences would be naive and superficial. While Geert Lovink, with his explicitly political and activist stance, has chosen to position himself outside social media, this text previously highlighted how Joshua Citarella's practices are grounded in performativity regarding online persona—exemplified for instance by the pursuit of Looksmaxxing while simultaneously producing theory about it. But what occurs when non-male critics attempt to publish their research online?

One of the most well-known and appreciated versions of virtual presence—the "Girl Online" currently widely portrayed in the media landscape—is often depicted as an aesthetically pleasing object of desire, rendering her an open and hospitable vessel for projected fantasies and market potential. Numerous writers and researchers have explored how the internet can host countless versions of this media figure, with a new version or alteration seemingly appearing each season. Often, this girl is represented through a naive, shallow, and non-informative lens—a perfect representation of societally constructed womanhood in a heteronormative and patriarchal hegemony. At times, the Girl Online may try to adopt a more assertive or less polished persona, but she ultimately returns to a softer or more palatable form, frequently rejecting the superficial benefits that capitalism offers. As researcher Sophie Publig argues in her interview on the podcast *Girl Employee*, this figure actually transcends gender categories. It functions more as a media archetype that facilitates the production of lifestyle, content, beauty, and, to some extent, knowledge. Through her aesthetic and consumerist tendencies, the Girl Online can gather a broad audience and sometimes penetrate through the shimmer of her own surface to deliver political stances or critical theories. As such, the Girl Online represents an ambiguous and complex concept that makes use of polarities as an often a successful strategy for attracting attention and engaging with others online.[117]

In the Wired article, "Everyone Is a Girl Online," Alex Quicho underlines how anyone who's attempting to present themselves online through an agency that goes beyond her aesthetics will be judged by haters who "will say that the girl has no access to individual agency and political autonomy, and is, therefore, an enemy of serious

117. Girl Employee, "Girl Online with Sophie Publig," accessed December 22, 2024, https://open.spotify.com/episode/5DUrPe8OFGM31MHEMTBkDD?si=m57qnTe4R8yLq_ONa0M1ug.

activism—or seriousness, at all. Lovers will reply that the girl is simply emptied of traditional humanist traits to make room for something else."[118] As emphasized by the theorist, in the post-platform and attention economy, a Girl Online does not decide whether or not she is perceived as such; she simply is. The performativity of girlhood, and its reception, whether it be silly, educational, sensitive, academic, or extremely rigid and scientific, cannot be understood outside of the scope of a "consumer category" that, as Alex Quicho argues, can't be delinked from capital. After all, it pays to be a Girl Online.[119] Although embodying the Girl Online might seem like a surrender: a passive acceptance of the rigid, oppressive structures she represents, deviating from her narrowly defined constraints exposes her to endless "correction" that may mean being sexualized, tokenized, or, most notably, not taken seriously—an issue less commonly experienced or perceived by those presenting as men online.

For many, performing the Girl Online is a strategic choice: she is an easily consumed item packaged in a format that the audience can easily recognize and engage with. In the long-form essay "Silly *Girl Theory*: Scrolling the Digital Playgrounds," Mela Miekus & Mita Medri present the various variations of girls online and display the many cards one can choose when introducing themselves as a girl online. They emphasize how "indeed, digital girlhood has been crafting online personas from the get-go. There was the Sad Girl who coped with her sadness through Tumblr mood boards or listening to Lana Del Rey. We also

118. Alex Quicho, "Everyone Is a Girl Online," *Wired*, September 11, 2023, https://www.wired.com/story/girls-online-culture/.
119. Polyester, "The Girl Is a Living Currency — How Womanhood Has Always Been Its Own Economy," *Polyester*, accessed December 22, 2024, https://www.polyesterzine.com/features/the-girl-is-a-living-currency-how-womanhood-has-always-been-its-own-economy.

saw the rise and fall of the Girlboss, who stormed the web with her CEO mentality and hustle culture grindset."[120] While their analysis focuses specifically on the lineage and aesthetic construction of the "silly girl", I propose to investigate the typology of the "Theory Girl", so to say, the girl online that produces theory. A subcultural trend already exists called "Dark Academia," an aesthetic that revolves around reading, writing, and learning. This vision of the dark, clever, and focused girl online who dwells in cold and dark libraries by candlelight can be at best described as a romanticization of an old, elitist, and past representations of educational experiences. As such, "Dark Academia" is merely a consumable aesthetic genre commodifying the experience of academia rather than a pathway towards delivering theoretical content.[121]

With enough searching, one can uncover a lineage and diversity of the "Theory Girl" online—a figure who may or may not intentionally embody this archetype. The theory girl could have remained a library rat who avoided conventional aesthetics and online presence, yet, like their counterpart, the Dark Academia girl, they understand the importance of performing intellectualism through visible traits and aesthetics to increase circulation and visibility online. She is a revered symbol and a sharp writer, thinker, and analyst - not only intelligent but also adept at curating the perfect image of herself and her work on the internet. Such figures are relevant idols to admire, as their careers already seem to be flourishing, whether in education, promotion, or fashion. As a result, they do not appear to need to bow to the demands

120. Mela Miekus and Mita Medri, "Silly Girl Theory: Scrolling the Digital Playgrounds," Blog, Institute of Network Cultures (blog), February 16, 2024, https://networkcultures.org/longform/2024/02/16/silly-girl-theory-scrolling-the-digital-playgrounds/.
121. Bateman Kristen, "Academia Lives — on TikTok," The New York Times, June 30, 2020, https://www.nytimes.com/2020/06/30/style/dark-academia-tiktok.html.

of algorithms on every platform. Their content, not always eager to please the platform tendencies, is perfect curation of memes, beauty, exciting research and events, and sometimes even lifestyle. Mindy Seu, Emily Segal, and Biz Sherbert or Bogna Konior exemplify the final stage of a Theory Girl online. But for theory girls online, all strategies and deliveries are welcome. Intellectual meme pages, such as the Instagram account @lacanadelrey or the TikTok account @nikitadumptruck (BimboUniversity), use static images and reels with a girl-coded aesthetic to present niche ideas or facts that might have otherwise gone unnoticed if not for their sugar-coated presentation.

The theory girls recognize that theory is not inherently suited for sharing or showcasing online. The theory girls also acknowledge that the format of their research—often long-form essays, articles, or perhaps even podcasts—may not align with the immediacy of online platforms. Yet, they know that being a girl online can serve as a vessel for delivering their message, allowing them to use the appeal of the "girl persona" or performance as an entry point to start sharing their ideas. Yet, they also understand that brand deals won't spontaneously appear, especially not from academic sources like JSTOR or Anna's Archive. As a result, theory girls have to be strategic and thoughtful, recognizing the limitations of platform-based criticism (with shadow-banning being one obvious constraint) and acknowledging that audiences primarily seek to be entertained or seduced—not lectured in a time of political urgency and climate crises. Additionally, the theory is that girls must tread carefully, for while audiences may appreciate a quirky girl, a nerdy girl, or a "not-like-the-other-girls" girl, still the online world often rejects those who express strong opinions. After all, the theory girls' aim isn't to create content that overtly claims to be intellectual; instead, they aim to build an audience that could ultimately engage with the many theories they have to offer some-where else. Therefore, any virtual intellectual presenting their research on social media may be required to engage in "online girl" performativity. In this context, being a the-ory girl online becomes a new stereotype and a strategy of displaying information, catching attention, and hoping to remain visible and relevant.

Beyond the Individual:
Towards a Third Collective Way?

Having acknowledged the potential decline of the traditional public intellectual and their transformation into a virtual figure, alongside the flattening of culture and the looming threat of the internet's collapse, what, if anything, endures? In a world dominated by mainstream culture, are we left with isolated enclaves of expertise and niche domains accessible to only a select few, from which new theories might emerge? Is the future of critical thinking destined to be scattered across individual Substack newsletters? In their book *After the Creator Economy*, the MetaLabel collective questions whether the ideology of knowledge production in the content-creation era is truly viable and sustainable: "For most people publishing creative work online, there is a growing sense of anxiety. While we have more online tools than ever to help operationalize and monetize creative businesses, the available options often feel mismatched with how we naturally create."[122] Indeed, while it appears that strategies of becoming a prosumer or a Girl Online seem indispensable for circulating one's voice today, such gestures mostly reinforce feelings of individuation, isolation, and competition when applied.

Returning to the primary figures of this research, it is crucial to emphasize that the practices of Geert Lovink

122. Austin Robey and Severin Matusek, eds., After the Creator Economy (Metabel Squad, 2024), 5.

and Joshua Citarella, while recognized as individual entities, seek to cultivate a network of thinkers and foster interactivity and connectivity through mailing lists, events, Discord channels, and meet-ups. These practices transcend notions of individuality, a concept also highlighted by Yancey Strickler in *The Dark Forest of the Internet*. The space in which the virtual intellectuals and the theory girls operate is not boundless and faces distinct limitations. Regardless of the individual's rewards, it does not take long for content creators to realize that the new rules they play with, although changed, can be equally restrictive and demanding.[123] Pressure to stay up-to-date, to post consistently, and to create or write on topics that ensure virality can take a toll on one's mental health in ways that go beyond any other imposed regularities. Yet, the initial desire, as written in *After the Creator Economy*, was "to share work in ways that feel right to us, not compete for attention on a feed."[124] Sometimes fooled by the new regulations of a platform (such as Patreon and their new taxation systems[125]), or shadow-banned for various reasons, content creators are, despite their privilege, often underlying the stressful conditions under which they have to work. In this context, Toby Corin suggests that this shift sparks a new conversation: "How should we be thinking about creative practices online—not as an 'economy,' but as an ecosystem?"[126]

In the essay "Post-Individual" featured in *After the Creator Economy*, Yancey Strickler envisions a digital age where individuality expands beyond the singular, and networks thrive as supportive and generous communities,

123. Emma Roth, "Patreon: Adding Apple's 30 Percent Tax Is the Price of Staying in the App Store," *The Verge*, August 12, 2024, https://www.theverge.com/2024/8/12/24218629/patreon-membership-ios-30-percent-apple-tax.
124. Austin Robey and Severin Matusek, eds., *After the Creator Economy* (Metabel Squad, 2024), 5.
125. Austin Robey and Severin Matusek, *After the Creator Economy*, 84.
126. Austin Robey and Severin Matusek, *After the Creator Economy*, 15.

aspiring to shape a new post-internet society. According to Severin Matusek, one of the contributors to the book, the internet, in its current form, cannot be sustained. The potential for harassment and negativity, as they exist, often dampens long-term desires to continue participating in such dialogues and economies.[127] As such, the book *After the Creator Economy* is a call for critical thinking beyond the commodification of the self in critical internet research, but for content creation online at large. It furthermore questions the limits of the existing models that are currently offering "freedom" for the margins. As cultural organizer Nati Linares ponders: "What would it look like if Patreon was not just a creator economy platform, but existed for collective mobilization? A resource hub for artist, social, and cultural movements?"[128] Consequently, this book challenges readers to envision a paradigm shift—from isolation to collaboration, content to context, and competition to cooperation. This raises critical questions: Is it possible to circumvent platform-driven content creation and algorithmic strategies to operate beyond the creator-individual model? Or must one first navigate the pathways to visibility and recognition before gaining the agency to influence and participate in change-making processes?

In *The Dark Forest Collective and The Dark Forest Anthology of the Internet* roundtable hosted by STOA, Joshua Citarella highlights how, in his own experience, platforms like Discord evolved into more meaningful sources of material and engagement.[129] The internet critic also notes how paywalls facilitated alternative forms of organization and how small-scale communities, such as *Do Not Research*, remained manageable. However, as

127. Austin Robey and Severin Matusek, *After the Creator Economy*, 46.
128. Austin Robey and Severin Matusek, *After the Creator Economy*, 59.
129. The Dark Forest Collective || *The Dark Forest Anthology of the Internet Roundtable*, Youtube Video, 2024, https://www.youtube.com/watch?v=QoyOE-_7dVQ&t=3264s.

Citarella and other internet critics have observed, what happens when platforms inevitably replicate these systems and subscription models? The challenge lies in finding pathways that transcend the extractive practices of platforms and their relentless efforts to commodify the creativity and community of every online participant. In this endeavor, only sustained dialogue and intentional public collaboration can foster approaches that preserve the analysis and evolution of the internet as a sustainable and equitable entity. A young, critical individual may lack the resources to drive such changes alone, but collectives and thinkers with greater social or financial capital have the voice and opportunity to create new institutions and opportunities.

Returning to critical internet research, how can we envision its future outside the extractive and strategic mechanisms of digital platforms? In *Internet Extinction*, Geert Lovink writes: "We know the state of disorder in the context of internet critique as the problem of information overload with its mental symptoms of distraction, exhaustion, and anxiety, precipitated by subliminal extractivist social media architectures."[130] In this light, critical internet research must resist despair when faced with the intricate challenges of creating, funding, and presenting research, as giving in would signify the triumph of platformization and extraction. In such a climate, fostering conversations, collaborations, and ongoing reassessment of the internet is essential, as is cultivating care. If "to experience the internet is to experience extinction,"[131] it is high time for us to collectively reclaim the digital spaces we inhabit, rethink our critiques, and remain hopeful in creating new theories, shaping new narratives, and building stronger

130. Geert Lovink, *Extinction Internet* (
    Institute of Network Cultures, 2022), 14.
131. Lovink, *Extinction Internet*, 35.

connections by using the best tools and available strategies. In this process, continuous conversations, collaborations, and alliances across generations will be essential. Critical thinking and the analysis of digital cultures and their platforms must remain dynamic, sustainable, and relevant. To do so, they must continuously evolve, change, and be scrutinized to effectively and broadly promote digital awareness and literacy.

Wrapping up this reflection, I recognize that many answers remain unexplored. For example, while creating alternative spaces for dialogue and critical thinking is valuable, what happens when the very platforms facilitating these encounters resort to shadow-banning or censoring the content they host? A reflection on this topic feels especially relevant as Meta and Instagram have demonstrated allyship with Trump's government, highlighting that social media platforms are far from neutral tools and that creators have limited ownership over their work. As it stands, platforms like TikTok, Instagram, and Patreon serve as a showcase, a library, and, for many artists, a portfolio, for thinkers, influencers, and content creators alike. As such, the dependence we have created on these tools, in pursuit of so-called "independence," seems to be coming back to haunt us. In this context, it will be crucial to shed more light on alternative, open-source social media platforms, with the hope that a gradual migration will take shape as awareness continues to grow.

Whether hosted on mainstream or alternative platforms, the rise of post-institutional organizations for critical research brings forth numerous challenges. As previously noted, a key element will be to avoid the trap of an individualistic, solitary model—one that romanticizes the precarious worker and assumes complex issues can be solved through the efforts of a few. The will to share, discuss, connect, collect, and collaborate must remain central for those projects to develop beyond personal interests. But once new models are established, how will we structure their growth to avoid replicating the systemic issues of gate-keeping, power dynamics, and limitations that plagued the institutions previously criticized? If we aim to sustain these alternatives as a cohesive archipelago, how can we ensure that they will collaborate rather than compete for resources or attention? Navigating these questions and tensions will be crucial for the future of internet research, as well as creative and critical thinking in its evolution.

↑   THE CRITICAL INTERNET RESEARCHER   ↑
AS A VIRTUAL INTELLECTUAL

↑   THE PROSUMER AS   ↑
CRITICAL INTERNET RESEARCHER

↑   THE RESEARCHER AS A PROSUMER   ↑

↑   THE ONLINE RESEARCHER   ↑

↑   THE ONLINE CONSUMER   ↑

TYPICAL TRAJECTORY OF CRITICAL
INTERNET RESEARCHERS

INTERVIEWS

Past and Future of the Critical Internet Researcher with Geert Lovink

Morgane: To start, could you please introduce yourself and share a bit about your practice?

Geert: Since 2004 I've been running the Institute of Network Cultures, a research group at the Polytechnic in Amsterdam, part of the Amsterdam University of Applied Sciences. This is a large institution with around 50,000 students. It's important to note that it shouldn't be confused with the University of Amsterdam, which is located nearby and also has about 50,000 students.

I've been developing this space within a tradition that I may have already begun in the early to mid-2000s. Before this, in 2002, I completed a PhD in Australia, focusing on critical internet culture. At the Institute of Network Cultures, we've built an extensive range of research networks, covering a variety of topics. These include search engines, critical Wikipedia studies, netporn, urban screens, ICT for Development and more.

We've also developed projects like MoneyLab, which explores revenue models in the arts, and *MyCreativity*, which examines working conditions in the creative industries. Our work addresses many facets of the digital landscape and its impact on society.

Morgane: Returning to the topic of the critical internet researcher, specifically, you and I, Geert, have discussed this concept and terminology extensively throughout my research. I'd like to ask if you could briefly summarize why you believe this term is particularly relevant to your practice and the work being developed at the Institute of Network Cultures.

Geert: Critical internet research originates from a project I worked on in 1994-95 with Pit Schultz, which culminated in the *nettime* mailing list. This platform, which has now existed for almost 30 years, was about interdisciplinary dialogue about internet criticism.

What is internet criticism? We're familiar with literary criticism, where people reflect on novels and literature, and film criticism, which dates back to the 1920s when this new medium emerged. There's extensive writing on the development of film language and how people analyze the culture and diversity of cinematic expression. Similarly, we can view the internet as a medium, much like theater, painting, visual culture, and other newer media like film, radio, and television. Since the 1990s, the internet has been added to that lineage.

Developing a critical vocabulary to analyze this medium is essential. It's a compelling idea and remains so today. But now, 30 years later, we must ask ourselves: What's left of that ideal? Is it still relevant? Can we still pursue independent critical internet research, whether outside or on the margins of academia? How does it relate to approaches in media and communication studies, law, sociology, political science, and other disciplines now engaging with the internet?

For us, critical internet research has always been situated within the arts and humanities. It's a project deeply tied to the agendas of visual artists, designers, and thinkers focused on aesthetics. That's a very specific perspective, and it's not one widely represented in mainstream academia. This is why we believe there's still a need for this approach.

Morgane: Moving on, there's another term that I think is highly relevant to this research: the concept of the virtual intellectual. You introduced this term in 1997 during a lecture, and I've used it in my argument to describe the figure of the rhetorical intellectual. Of course, the concept of the virtual intellectual extends beyond critical internet researchers, it can apply to many figures in political science and beyond. Essentially, it encompasses anyone seeking to establish a platform and maintain a presence online, especially in today's social media-driven world. When you introduced the concept of the virtual intellectual back in 1997, could you share what you had envisioned at the time? What led you to understand this transition from a faceless or anonymous intellectual to a persona that would need to exist in media and online spaces?

Geert: My thinking about the role of the intellectual has been deeply influenced by my time and activities in the former Soviet Union and Central and Eastern Europe—before, during, and particularly after the fall of the Berlin Wall in 1989 and the collapse of the Soviet Union in 1991. I was very much a part of those changes.

In Eastern Europe, there was always a specific understanding of what it meant to be an intellectual: someone with societal responsibilities, not necessarily as a dissident but as a figure tasked with reflecting on the production of ideas within social, aesthetic, and political economies. This concept of intellectual responsibility was very potent for me, particularly as new media began to grow.

At that time, speculative concepts were becoming increasingly important. We recognized that ideas and concepts weren't neutral...They could grow and spread virally, shaping networks, products, platforms, and, ultimately, power structures. This awareness was already present in the language of the 1990s. Don't forget that the term "meme," popularized by Richard Dawkins, was conceptualized long before that era.

These rapid technological developments, from the introduction of personal computers to mobile phones, smartphones, virtual communities, blogs, social networking, and social media, highlighted the power of ideas and their role in shaping these changes. It became clear to me that intellectuals had a unique opportunity to engage with and influence this transformation.

This proposition was shaped by a very European, or even Central European, perspective. By the 1990s, with the rise of venture capital, Silicon Valley, and neoliberalism, the role of shaping these ideas was often attributed to entrepreneurs. But we must ask: where do entrepreneurs get their ideas from? This brings us back to the role of programmers, designers, artists, theorists, critics, and intellectuals.

In my 1997 essay, I contrasted this emerging role of the 'virtual' intellectual with what I referred to as the *Gutenberg intellectual.* This older archetype had been around for at least 500 years, tied to the rise of the printing press and the subsequent development of books, libraries, bookshops, newspapers, magazines, coffeehouses, and the public sphere. By the 1990s, it was evident that this paper-centric public sphere was fading. While media like radio, film, and television had already begun centralizing public discourse, they were still largely inaccessible to individual producers. However, with the advent of the computer, media production began to democratize, granting far more people access to the means of creating critical discourse and new concepts. This shift formed the basis of my 1997 proposition on the virtual intellectual.

Morgane: Do you consider yourself a virtual intellectual in this sense, particularly because of the creation and proliferation of content produced by the Institute of Network Cultures?

Geert: I haven't revisited the notion of the intellectual since 1997. I'm not entirely sure why...that's a good question. Perhaps it felt a bit pretentious, or maybe it was because I didn't see the specific class I had in mind emerging.

The idea of class, or of becoming a class, is significant here. Intellectuals form a certain social group, and whether or not they constitute a class in themselves is still debatable. This was a question people actively discussed in the early 20th century. I remember a book by Arthur Kroker and Michael Weinstein called *The Virtual Class*, published in 1993. These two postmodern Canadian thinkers explored the idea of a virtual class, but not so much in terms of the internet and networks as we think of them today. They were focused more on virtual reality. I always found that perspective puzzling, but they took the idea of a new class composition seriously.

Over time, I've adjusted and refined this idea. I've shifted focus toward the role of the theorist as a producer of concepts, and even more specifically, the role of the critic—someone who reflects on the logic of culture to anticipate and debate its future.

Today, this practice is widespread. Many people, especially in recent weeks, engage in what I once referred to as internet criticism. Just think about the countless voices commenting on Elon Musk, the changes made by Mark Zuckerberg, or the broader shifts toward figures like Trump. All of this falls under the rubric of internet criticism, a framework that has become increasingly relevant.

Morgane: What would you say makes a virtual intellectual successful in this context? How would you define success for a virtual intellectual today?

Geert: That's very clear, and it's not so hard to measure. I think the ultimate test is this: is he or she able to introduce and follow up on a viable concept?

Take something like *Girl Theory*, for instance. Where does that come from? Who invented it? It's a very potent idea. A lot of people immediately respond to it, not just girls in the narrow sense, but a much broader audience. People relate to it deeply.

This demonstrates the power of a productive, critical concept. It's not only reflecting on the culture at large, especially as we see it on social media, but it's also a proposition. From as early as 1997, I've seen it as the task of the virtual intellectual to produce these kinds of concepts.

These concepts should have two key elements: on the one hand, they should be imaginative, perhaps even utopian or speculative. On the other hand, they must also be critical and grounded in a deep reflection on the dominant culture. Girl Theory embodies both of these aspects, making it a great example of a successful critical concept.

Morgane: I'll dive deeper into it with Alex Quicho and Sophie Publig at a later moment in this project. What I would also argue now is that what makes virtual intellectuals sustainable in their work is the active circulation of their practice. This leads me to ask you about the Institute of Network Cultures, as it is currently entering a period of transition with organizational shifts and questions about sustainability.

As you approach retirement, how do you envision the agency of the Institute evolving and thriving in the future? Will it take on a different shape than what has been, let's say - "institutionalized" to some extent?

Morgane: You became the institution!

Geert: That's right. I was very clear about this then because, you know, coming from the squatter and autonomous movements, the idea of having an institute still feels a bit ironic. I still laugh at the title even after 20 years because, yes, we are clearly not doing what people might assume an institute would do.

And still, we are embedded within this large school, which funds about 3 or 4 of our jobs. We're not a huge institution, but it's a privilege to have these resources. Nonetheless, many of our projects rely on external funding. The school doesn't finance all of them. So, while some basic support has been in place for the past 20 years, the actual activities require securing budgets from various sources—sometimes even operating without funding, which has its challenges. In the last 3, 4, or 5 years, I haven't had much funding, especially as our research has become increasingly marginal. Many of the funding bodies are less inclined to support our work. In that sense, we've found ourselves, ironically, back at square one.

Morgane: When thinking about independent platforms for critical thinking, I've referenced the Institute of Network Culture in this project, comparing it to *Do Not Research.* It seems that *Do Not Research* has set out to be and managed to remain non-institutionalized. The project survives through the participation of writers who volunteer or receive a small fee, as well as through micropayments or other more regular payment sources like Substack. Do you see independent practices and platforms like *Do Not Research* as the future for virtual intellectuals in general, and more specifically, for critical internet researchers?

Geert: This is an idea that's been around for quite some time. If you trace it back to the very beginning, I did an interview in 1992, which you can find on archive.org, discussing micropayments and the early digital cash projects here in Amsterdam. These are considered to be some of the earliest roots of Bitcoin and the entire crypto movement. So, these ideas have already been circulating here for quite a while. It became clear early on that state funding wouldn't be available for these initiatives, which led to the realization that you'd have to find a way to organize funding on your own. We were already doing this in the squatter movement in the 1980s. My master's thesis in Political Science at the University of Amsterdam in 1983 was about how autonomous media projects, as part of the squatter movement, financed themselves. So, this question has been on the table for a long time.

This situation is evolving, and I hope we'll see technological advancements in the coming years and decades, as they're needed right now. We're currently seeing the dominance of the influencer model, where influencers are primarily paid through advertisements and small payments, mostly from companies like Meta, Google, and maybe a few other platforms. I've always held a utopian vision where we wouldn't need these platforms. That's a bit of my naive 1990s background when we believed payments could be made directly—just from you to me—without intermediaries. I'd love to see more experimentation in that area. Of course, this was one of the original promises of Bitcoin and the crypto world. However, it's largely shifted in another direction towards speculation as an end goal, rather than developing into micropayment systems. But who knows? Maybe in the next iteration, this could happen.

Morgane: Speaking about the future of collective organization, particularly in the speculative field of critical internet research—whether for the Institute of Network Cultures, *Do Not Research*, or more generally—I'd like to ask you, given your career and experience with self-organization and independent practices, what do you think is essential for people of our generation to organize collectively? How can we continue to build supportive collaborations in this precarious and, let's say, unstable state we find ourselves in?

Geert: We [the Institute of Network Cultures] want to demonstrate that self-organization can be incredibly powerful. This is important because, in the liberal, neoliberal, or libertarian models of social media, the focus is always on the individual—the idea that each person has to organize everything for themselves. We never believed that would be a sustainable model,

and it turns out only very few people manage to succeed under it. If you look at the influencer model,
you'll see that there are very few influencers and only
a handful can truly thrive. The model itself only creates a small number of successful entrepreneurs.

As a result, the system, as it is structured now,
ends up creating monopolies, with a small group of
people earning large amounts of money, while most
others can't make a living from their work. This forces
people to take on day jobs and then spend their eve-
nings as bloggers, podcasters, etc. This has been the
reality over the past two decades, and it's precisely
the kind of model we didn't want. We envisioned a
more horizontal, decentralized, federated system of
income distribution and generation. We still believe
that's possible. However, as history may show, that
can only be achieved if we do it together—through
cooperatives, collectives, or organized networks.
It might even be seen as a trade union approach,
though I'm not sure exactly what to call it. But fundamentally, it's a social approach—the idea that income
can only be secured and sustained if it's generated in
a social context.

Morgane: What do you think are the biggest challenges
or obstacles we're facing in trying to develop these platforms? We've seen that sometimes, early experiments or
projects get started but never truly come to fruition. What
do you think are the biggest obstacles, or "brakes," one
might encounter when it comes to not just initiating such
initiatives, but making them succeed?

Geert: There's always money to be made in trend-
watching consultancy or think tank-type activities,
working as consultants for the corporate world.

That's what most people do, and it's still where most of the money is made. However, the crypto world, despite what you may think about it, has already shown that it can create value by itself. It's not just taking value from the corporate world or anything like that. While I'm not interested in copying that model, I do think it offers some inspiration because it shows that it is possible to create alternative revenue sources. That's something we should aim for.

Of course, there are other models that *Money Lab* has been looking at, such as the subscription model, which you're also researching. Another option is platforms like *Kickstarter*, which could be seen as a form of distributed, socialized venture capital. You ask others to take a risk with you to help build something or at least sustain your living costs while you're engaged in a project. This could apply to anything, whether it's a personal project, an NGO, a social movement, or an aesthetic practice—it doesn't matter.

So, there are more possibilities. As the traditional corporate world collapses, people will seek out alternative forms of income. Of course, maybe some people believe the world is doomed and everything will collapse, but even then, people will still find ways to develop these models, though perhaps under very different and darker circumstances. A random example is the people in L.A. who had to survive after tens of thousands of homes were burned down. They immediately turned to crowdfunding to meet their basic needs and then, of course, to raise money for rebuilding.

Morgane: I'd like to end this interview by revisiting a question I asked you at the very beginning of this research process when we first started discussing this entire topic. I asked you about a book that covers the history of critical internet research, particularly when it's done on the margins, and you mentioned that such a book doesn't exist. I also asked if you planned on writing it one day, and I'd like to ask you that again, as we conclude this interview.

Geert: I do intend to, write more about the 1990s again, and I'm in the process of collecting the necessary stories. Due to my retirement, I'll be stepping down from my work here at the institute, and then I plan to start writing the book. In the past, I worked with Adilkno, and we wrote the history of the Amsterdam squatters movement in English, called *Cracking the Movement*. That covered the 1980s, and I intend to write something similar about the 90s. We need these historical writings, and we could wait for other historians, but in my experience, that's a bit of a waste. There's also this element that Bernard Stiegler has declared, and the late French philosopher emphasized, which is that it's also our task to ensure that knowledge and theory—production and reflection— are packaged in a way that can be passed on to the next generation.

This is a responsibility: not just an educational one, but also a theoretical and reflective task in itself. It's about thinking long-term and sharing our experiences, regardless of whether they were failures or – you know, even though they might be romantic – inspiring, or bitter. It's all part of it. And yes, I believe it's important to pass on the experiences of the first 30 years of the internet to the next generation.

Building Platforms for Critical Internet Researchers with Joshua Citarella

Morgane: Joshua, could you introduce yourself?

Joshua: First, I should say I'm a huge fan of your writing, which I have followed for several years. We've published a few of your pieces on *Do Not Research*, and yes, I'm very excited to talk about all of these things.

I think people probably know me now mostly through my podcasts, my presence on the internet, my newsletters, and so on. Before that, I had a ten-plus-year track record of participating in gallery shows and museums, coming from the capital-A professional art world. I still have a presence there—I'm showing in, I don't know, maybe five different museum shows in Europe right now. I'm more active than ever, but quantitatively speaking, my audience is just overwhelmingly on the platforms.

People probably know me as a podcaster more than they do an artist at this point, which has been a kind of interesting and relevant evolution for, I think, some of the stuff we'll talk about today.

I'm also the founder of an arts organization called *Do Not Research*, which began as a private Discord community that gathered to discuss internet politics and mimetic influence during a critical period when those topics were largely unexplored by existing institutional structures. I guess we're now starting year four of that project, where we publish at least once a week. We have approximately 300 different contributors. There's a wide gamut of material that comes out of there, but generally, it's about internet culture, its political influence, and all of these super interesting topics that I'm sure we'll dive into today.

Morgane: I would like to go back to what can be read in your bio, either on your website or on Instagram. You use the term "internet critic," and I would like you to perhaps tell me why you chose this term and how it relates to your practice.

Joshua: I don't think we have great terms for this particular position that has opened up in the last few years because we're not exactly influencers. I would say that this applies to maybe myself and the *New Models* podcast specifically.

Several people have kind of moved from the art world to—I guess, on your tax return it says that you're a content creator or something. On the platforms, practically speaking, you are posting to *YouTube* or *Substack*. This also applies to the artist Brad Troemel for example, who's a longtime friend and collaborator of mine.

These are people who are working at a relatively high level of discourse that would normally be discussed in the context of the academy, but they're doing it out on the platforms. They have these crowd-funded, subscriber-supported projects, which are quite different from those produced by regular content creators that you may come across. The audiences are relatively smaller, they are embedded in more niche intellectual discussions outside of the academy proper.

We don't have a great term for it because it's something that developed relatively recently. And how would you delineate someone who's an influencer on *TikTok* versus an intellectual who happens to be publishing on *Substack*? Those are just new classifications without clear institutional delineations nor affiliations or anything like that.

The general framing of platforms versus institutions is something I keep returning to. We are experiencing a process where a lot of institutional structures are just being liquidated, unfortunately, through the adjunctification of higher education. This trend is far more pronounced in the States than in Europe.

But yeah, I've fluctuated between a few different roles. I generally introduce myself as an artist and internet culture writer. Now, people – maybe more so – know me as a podcaster. But my friend, Brad [Troemel], would always say that art is the one professional field that does not abide by the disciplines of any other field, meaning that it allows for whatever you want to do.

If you're a journalist or a scientist, or if you're working in media theory—there's no system of peer review in the arts. Artists are encouraged to make weird, agnostic connections and get very adventurous with their thinking. I think art is a very generative, important place in society where you can come up with new things that can't easily be categorized. That's what I think is exciting about it.

Morgane: Internet criticism, as you practice it online, somehow resonates with the concept of the Virtual Intellectual introduced by Geert [Lovink] in the '90s. Already in 1997, he held a lecture in which he described the virtual intellectual as a person who uses aesthetics and social strategy to effectively deliver their ideas—of course, while relying on micropayments and multiple visibility channels. One can find the lecture in the archives of the *<nettime>* mailing list. Do you identify with this figure? And what would you say makes the difference between being a virtual intellectual and being an influencer?

Joshua: I would say Geert Lovink's work is an inspiration and something formative to my education. He is one of the few people we were able to read in this very niche circle of art and tech. One of the things I value about those fields is the time-stamping of ideas that are far ahead of the curve, right?

The idea that there would be a virtual intellectual probably seemed a little bit outside of the Overton Window or the realm of possibilities at the time when it was first published. But today, it is an existing reality. I happen to be living it—for better or worse. Until social media was introduced, along with crowdfunded sites such as Patreon and Substack, and the practical building of the infrastructure for these things, it wasn't yet possible to realize in a practical sense what was possible to theorize.

I try to take a similar approach now when I talk about social media and building grassroots political movements that are organized through these media channels. I think the game we're playing here—this kind of data trend-casting or tech-cultural trend-casting—is about what these tools can lead to.

If the communicative infrastructure exists, the network exists, and the possibility to send payments exists, one could theorize many years ahead of time that figures like this would emerge in some capacity, whether those are influencers, intellectuals, or what have you. I take a tremendous amount of inspiration from those ideas.

This is the education I was given in the art world: I'm looking at a set of tools right now, which is a giant spreadsheet, usually a CSV file, of people. It's got their names, their contact info, their phone numbers. They're sending payments and supporting these big media networks that infrequently propose calls to action. For example, people will go and canvass for candidates, and they will get practically involved in electoral politics.

To me, that looks structurally and diagrammatically very similar to what regular existing political organizations do. They use the same tools: in one case those are being deployed for sending a newsletter or a podcast, and in another case, to – through a different type of newsletter– mobilize people to canvass and so on.

I'm hypothesizing–based on the type of education I was given–that these tools can be deployed for a whole set of reasons. And we may expect that they will be used for different reasons in the future. Those are the values and the type of analysis I was taught to bring to technology, which comes from people like Geert.

Morgane: In my research, I argued that *Do Not Research,* much like the Institute of Network Cultures, which was founded by Geert Lovink, enables discourse that cannot easily thrive on institutional platforms. Is this something you'd agree with? If you could answer this by giving us a brief history and context of how *Do Not Research* came to life, that would be very useful.

Joshua: You're just bringing up my favorite topic to rant about in the whole world, I could easily go off on that. Maybe the kind of formative example I always give is: in 2018, I published a long-form essay—about

10,000 of my own words, plus 10,000 words from people in these memetic subcultures. It was an ethnographic overview of this radical meme community, generally composed of people between the ages of 12 and 17, who were posting pretty radical stuff—in some cases, pretty dangerous or reprehensible content.

No existing institution in the art world wanted to publish it, not even for free. People were simply not interested in this work whatsoever. They were afraid of it because, at the time, looking at memes and internet culture was conflated with fascism, even though the people I was writing about were from the left. Just touching on the topic of memes, in general, was terrifying to these institutions. I decided to bypass the gatekeepers and put my work on the platforms. And lo and behold, there were a lot of people who were interested in this stuff. It's the only document of its kind. It's been six years now, and there's still no other ethnography that is as detailed and has that level of access.

It turns out that it was quite historically significant. It was also a profitable thing to publish, which is unusual for this type of research. There were so many people interested in it that some of them chose to financially support the project to facilitate more work like that.

To me, that was such a clear example that there was important work to be done within the intellectual lineage of the art world that just wasn't being supported by the existing institutional structures.

The problem you then run into is that when you're publishing on the platforms, there's the threat of getting deplatformed or shadow-banned, and so on. Shortly after I published the book —maybe about a year later—both Brad Troemel and I hit this at the same time. We spent, if I recall correctly, about six months in a shadow ban that stripped us of 90% of our audience.

That's a significant problem if you've bypassed the gatekeepers but are now effectively otherwise muted or silenced in your ability to publish. It was tremendously expensive. Honestly, this time was crippling financially because you couldn't reach all the people who were actively trying to support your work, even if you were proposing a better narrative and weren't part of the dangerous communities you were commenting on.

In some cases, sheerly by commenting on the piece or republishing it—even in a critical capacity— other users were devastated, muted, and silenced by the platforms. What you have to come up with is a protected space where you can have contextual discussions and not risk losing your ability to reach your audience.

And my God, we're describing institutions again. Through this process, I think you kind of reason your way through: the existing institutional structures may not be the vehicle we want to use, but the platforms are not a good alternative either. You can lose your audience there. There are parameters for political speech, and we need spaces where we can have rich, contextual discussions and talk about things that may have a risk when deployed at scale for society. But experts need to be able to confer, produce analysis on those things, do agenda-setting, and produce a kind of qualitative research that would guide how journalists and the platforms should interpret some of this stuff.

As one possible example of this—and this is a bit of an anecdote: a good friend of mine, who came from the art world, worked in one of these think tanks and produced a policy paper that was then read by the head of Twitter at the time. This paper informed a lot of his decisions about how to interpret irony posting. This is someone who, from the art academy, leveraged their expertise in the field of aesthetics and semiotics. And then that became the practical policy for how to interpret someone posting a *Pepe* meme, for example. His paper was used to determine whether that was an image from an extremist group or just a harmless piece of internet culture. The direct application of the theory we learn in media studies is more relevant than ever.

In terms of *Do Not Research*: there's a wide range of material that comes through it. But we are in the process of starting year four, and we are nearly registering as an A5A1C3 organization, which is the official nonprofit status in the United States. We've published contributions from something like 300 different contributors. I need to take a final count because we just brought in the next year of our programming. But this is about recreating these institutional structures in a meaningful sense. DNR gives grants, awards honorariums to contributors, promotes people's work, and creates the context through which to understand the things they're publishing.

I think a lot of that approach was informed by my education in the art world, which came from the world of Capital P photography at that time, an era when photography bled into new media. Around that era, Photoshop had come out, and the internet was new. But essential to my education was the idea that, over the 20th century, existing institutional structures didn't have a photography department. They had printmaking, painting, sculpture, and other departments, but there were no photo curators, and museums didn't collect photography, for example.

Over the 20th century, these arguments were rigorously made, and the aesthetic and cultural impact of this medium was argued effectively. People produced indisputably great masterworks—artworks that were representative of the cultural values at that time. Museums eventually opened photography departments as a result, meaning that something that was once outside the institutional structures was then metabolized and brought into them.

Resources from institutions were allocated towards photography: scarce wall space in museums, programming, and publishing schedules were all allocated to photography. This thing proved its relevance. I've always thought of that as an example of what we are supposed to do as a media theory avant-garde: make the argument about why these things are important, and how they affect culture, and then we, ourselves, would be similarly metabolized into the existing institutional structures for a variety of reasons.

That seems to have broken down, though. Art is now totally disconnected from everyday life, and internet culture, and seemingly completely irrelevant and conservative. It has backed itself into this weird kitsch corner, which is hopefully on a path toward correction. I would say that's the long arc of *Do Not Research* and my thoughts on platforms and what we're trying to build in the next few years.

Morgane: Based on your practice, your internet research projects, and your broader perspective of forecasting something outside of institutions that eventually gets metabolized into them, what do you envision for the future of internet criticism and media studies?

Joshua: I think I'm a little bit of a pessimist on this. I've been thinking about it this week because a friend of the podcast, Daniel Keller, is doing a talk at MoMA with the Ambasz Institute. I did a talk there in the summer, I believe it was June. There are these moments where people who have worked outside of the institution are being invited in, given a platform, published, and their opinions are being heard. I think that these institutional structures are, for a variety of political and macroeconomic reasons, just in a state of decline right now. What I anticipate happening is this kind of flourishing Balkanization—an archipelago of many small, competing institutions. I think this is more of an institutional lifecycle thing, where over the next few years, we're going to see a lot of small magazines crop up.

We've got that very much happening in downtown New York, which is where young, creative people tend to gather. There are these small formations of people building competing structures, let's say. I believe Artforum, similarly, is a legacy publication, maybe the foremost centralized authority of what constituted the professional art world, and it does indeed seem to be on the decline in a way that may not be repairable for another generation, after the fallout with Penske Media and letting go of so much staff, and just the reputational damage among the community.

It's good to participate in these legacy structures, but I also really feel like unless you're building a life raft and have an exit plan, you will go down with the ship for most of these things. I maybe felt differently a few years ago, when our job was to kind of course-correct the Titanic, grip the wheel, and try to avert the iceberg. But I believe there are too many things in motion now where exit has kind of become unavoidable and necessary.

The thing that I like to harp on is: make sure that your exit is not just to the platforms or that you're doing the libertarians' dirty work for them. Make sure your exit is to some new institutional structure, such as a magazine, a curated space, or a group of people who are working together around a shared set of values.

Morgane: Funny anecdote—back in 2019, I was living in New York while doing an exchange at Cooper Union. That's actually where I first came across your work. My roommate, who knew I was interested in institutional criticism, sent me one of your Instagram posts. In it, you talked about your disappointment with the institutional setting and your teaching position, how you found it overly reductive, and that you wanted to fully commit to being online as an influencer. Looking back on that statement from five years ago, and considering how successful your work and research have been since, how do you view that decision now?

Joshua: Yeah, yeah. No, that's—I mean, that piece comes up a lot. It's especially relevant because I did, in fact, after probably 4 or 5 years away, just teach a semester for one class at RISD, the Rhode Island School of Design, which is an institution I feel very close to and I have a lot of colleagues and friends there. I have conflicting feelings about it because, one, I feel that particular statement I made was interpreted as a call to action for people who are within the institutional structures to set out and launch their careers as influencers and content creators.

I just want to highlight that unless you had these specific conditions of being probably part of post-Internet art, had an existing following that wanted to support your work and were making work in the type of genre and topics that people such as Brad, myself, and *New Models* were making work about, I think that it's not financially possible for a lot of people. But what happened at that time was interesting. In the later portion of that open letter that I posted—a screenshot of the notes app that I put up on Instagram at that time, I mention that in a previous model of American society and intellectual discourse, the way that you would access resources–meaning: get paid– but also could publish to an audience, was gated through institutions. But those institutions had sets of values, they had all of the resources behind these walls. Then there was a moat with a narrow drawbridge that everybody had to walk over and say, "These values are so great", "I love everything you do here", or "This institution is wonderful." Then it gave you a big check at the end of it, and you could do whatever kind of work you were getting up to.

What started to happen while publishing in the old institutional structures of museums and magazines and so on, but then also publishing on my own Substack and Patreon and whatever crowdfunded context, is that I could measure the amount of revenue that I was getting from posting the same text in either case. What happened was that the crowdfunding eclipsed the amount of money that I would get paid from the magazines or the museums. This made it clear to me that part of the fragmentation into these counter-elite structures, the backlash to wokeness, and just all of the things that were rebelling against the values of the institutional structures at the time, formed in some way a question of the institution's inability to discipline its workforce. There were no longer heavy enough incentives for people to play by its rules. If people could break off from the legacy structures and maintain the same low level of income, the incentives at that time were split. I think the way that I phrased it in the piece was that the institutions pay below market rate for their work, and that is meaningful. This can, in some cases, get people excited that we're going to rebel against corrupt institutions or whatever. But we should be equally aware that this movement has also really benefited right-wing people who choose to rebel against the institutional values and start their contrarian edge lord-Substack, or something nonsensical like that. So, yes. It may not always work out for the best, but I think that we're kind of watching that play out.

This is sometimes called "bundling." You go through different media cycles where independent writers will bundle their work together into a new magazine, and then at a certain point, someone will break off from the magazine and start their independent project. There's kind of this sine curve, right? There are peaks and valleys in which the creative industry is bundled together in the form of, for example, a record label, and then people break apart and do their solo practices. I think we're watching an elongated process of that happen with the legacy institutional structures as well. We are in this kind of downward cycle at the bottom of the sine curve, in which the institutional structures have fewer resources and just quantitatively speaking, less reach. If you go on MSNBC, you talk to fewer people than on the Joe Rogan podcast, for example. We're seeing a quantitative order of magnitude, a kind of similar asymmetry to how Brad Troemel must speak to ten times the audience of *Spike* magazine... Sorry to single out Spike magazine. I like their publication, just at some point, it is a numbers game for audience and influence. Those things lay out a pretty big landscape that we haven't seen before in the previous generations. Just how will people respond to that? We're just on the early side of this trend cycle trying to produce this new magazine label-type structure. That's going to be the story of our professional lives for the next five to ten years: trying to navigate that sine curve, bundling and bundling.

Morgane: There's a critique I've raised in my writing, which is that starting and sustaining something like a presence on Substack or a similar platform requires a very specific type of network and visibility from the outset. The idea of going from zero to a thousand subscribers, for example, often feels like an overpromised dream sold to many today.. While it's fantastic that these platforms encourage people to create their vitrines, how realistic is that dream of finding success in this way for most?

Joshua: Right, that's immensely important. I don't want people to interpret that statement I made, as they often do, that this is a call for everyone to take this path because there are a lot of things that need to line up to make that even possible. Maybe the most important thing to say is that from the period of post-Internet art in which people like myself and Brad started our careers, we both graduated in 2010 and had solo shows in 2013. By 2012, we were working as full-time artists – meaning that we had a place to live, a separate studio in which we made work that was sold by galleries, and that's how we made a living – that is a very anomalous, weird path that did not exist for the generation of artists before us, such as the Josh Klines of this world and so on. People who are just ten years older didn't have a two-year arc of graduating, having a practice, and then immediately going into the market. What combined to produce that type of effect was, for one, social media, which bypassed the institutional gatekeepers and remapped visibility within the art world.

It started this competitive dynamic between collectors which made the underlying social contacts visible to people. It could create really big hype cycles around work. There were websites dedicated to charting speculative valuations of work coming out at that time. I had a friend whose work—maybe I won't mention his name, but he was priced at $400 in 2010, $4,000 in 2012, and $40,000 in 2014. That increase of two orders of magnitude is a clear indication of an unsustainable bubble. What had happened around that time when social media was remapping visibility is that all of the money from the 2008 financial crisis a few years earlier had drifted upwards and enriched this new collector class, which was very interested in kind of flipping artworks, and speculative bubbles. They were interested in culture, but they were also interested in the prestige and the money around it.

For a while, that kind of floated all of the boats. You had artists that were engaging with populist topics, in that we were reaching wide audiences and making viral posts on Tumblr and stuff. That's how we bootstrapped our careers. But then we were immediately plucked up from that into this super luxury market where art was treated as a financial asset. Unless that had happened at that specific time with those specific topics, it would not have. I don't think that there's another similar path now. The only thing like that that has happened, similarly because of speculative bubbles, is that maybe some 15-year-old made wacky NFTs and their stuff blew up. I try to follow this stuff a little bit, but I'm not well-versed in it. I don't think that that particular set of conditions is happening again in the art world, at least as I've seen it for the last 15 years at this point.

Morgane: Coming back to, let's say, more critical thinking and making: as someone who navigates between public and private, institutional and marginal spaces, what is the most significant insight you've gained about critical thinking and creative production?

Joshua: I'm going to try and choose my words carefully on this one because it's a little bit of a dark topic, I guess. I go through a lot of submissions for *Do Not Research*. We will get something like 400 submissions, and the project will continue to grow. Although I am not teaching in a wide capacity right now, I do have a general sense of what young creative people are up to, of what is representative of that type of work; the references and citations they make, and the topics they choose to write about. I also have access to the quantitative numbers on Substack, which are always opaque to the tributaries to *Do Not Research* because those incentives of the network and attention are not the things that we want to promote, but I am aware of them. I see the type of work that young people are producing, the context in which they were educated, the citations that they produce, and then just how those things actually in a meaningful sense resonate with the audience of people, their peers, who they're speaking to.

The thing that I've observed is that a lot of the education people were given in these academies enshrined a set of values that people learned to mimic the effect of the court for their upward mobility within those institutions. What I mean by that is that young people would go to these academies, universities, whatever, and they would learn to reproduce the language and affect of people who had high-status positions, they may or may not believe those things, and their peers may or may not believe those things, and when allowed to voluntarily engage with those values and priorities, people may just choose to opt-out.

And all of that is the result of this moat model of the institution, where unless you espouse those values, that particular canon, you're not allowed to walk over the drawbridge. But as the resources have seeped out the sides of these fortresses and they're just kind of liquidated out on the platforms, there's not the same incentive to fall in line with those beliefs and values. There's been this proliferation of different competing structures that skew left and skew right. I think we're watching — this is a bad sign for the life cycle of an institution — when the young people who participate in it merely espouse the values to advance their careers, but they do not meaningfully believe them. When they are allowed to voluntarily engage or reproduce those things, or even drop financial support, or a comment, people just aren't choosing to do it.

Benjamin Bratton calls this boomer theory. This is a theory of media and culture that was largely propagated by tenured professors who grew up during the postwar boom. All they want to do is talk about dismantling corrupt institutions and whatever, whatever it is that they're getting up to — the most spoiled generation in the history of the world. This is just not scaling to the lived experience of millennials and Zoomers, who now have a different set of values. It's been an interesting period to see how some of those things go out to a real audience of their peers, of the people who they would want to be talking to, building alongside, and creating the new world with. Those people just don't care about the stuff that's taught in the academies very often. That's been personally a very difficult thing to contemplate, where I absorbed a lot of things that I thought were important ideas within the canon of both media theory and aesthetics and whatever. A lot of those things, once liberated — once you take the blinders off — you realize... It was not important at all. That was just a lot of really wealthy people who had the resources all to themselves, and they were extracting rents from young creatives. That's the way the whole model worked.

Once there's an opportunity to seek your ability to publish in your resources, why are you going to stick in an old system that's just extracting rent and labor from you? The downward decline, the crumbling of these institutional structures is, I think, something to in some cases celebrate because it has been at the debt — the indebtedness — of the emerging creative generation, which is, I think, a great crime. I have literally — this is, I won't say the name of the institution — literally paid rent to rent works from existing institutions for canon, the canon of artists who have, untold, unfathomable wealth that should be just loaned out to young emerging artists for free if they're willing to put in the labor. These structures are very, very much exploitative and corrupt.

Morgane: It makes me curious if you have any short thoughts on what, then, you can assume from *Do Not Research* from the pieces that I see being written and shared, and like that, we have a little bit of a similar repertoire. So, what do you see appearing as a new canon?

Joshua: This is exactly the problem. If you're departing from the institutional structures and you're saying

that this stuff is bad and corrupt, and you're not proposing any alternative or positing a set of values,
then, well, what the hell are you doing? It is then in-
cumbent upon you, in building these new institutional
structures, to highlight the parts of the canon, the
ideas, the artists, and the work specifically that you
think are worth valorizing and historicizing.

What we do as part of *Do Not Research* is, every
year, we do a handful of these artist profiles to build a
canon to educate, influence, and create a kind of historical lineage with the participation of these artists
from previous generations. Just to highlight a few of
those: Last year, we did a profile on the artist Trevor
Paglen, who was an immense inspiration to me, is
very fond, and a huge supporter of *Do Not Research*.
We talked to Dina Jago, who was a founding member of K-Hole, an incredibly influential trend-casting
group. Her work is now in the Museum of Modern Art
and many other places I can't even name. She's had a
tremendously successful career. Simon Denny, artist,
friend, and supporter of *Do Not Research* — we did a
profile on him in the previous year. Our art cycle for
the next few months is going to be a profile on New
Models: Carly Busta. I think New Models is maybe the
Berlin version of *Do Not Research*. Carly Busta was
previously at Artforum and then Techstars or Kunst in
Berlin. She left to build this new structure to have her
publishing platform, podcast, and website.

We're also going to talk to DIS, which was maybe
the first example of the failure of institutional metab-
olism, where after they curated the Berlin Biennial,
they were not invited to become, for example, video
curators of whatever, or any other institution. They
were the tastemakers of an entire generation of
post-internet art. And no one wanted to absorb them

into their model, even though it was wildly popular, successful, and had institutional credibility. They created a site called DIS Art that now has, I can't even imagine, thousands of hours of artist videos behind a very minor paywall, which is unlocked by being a student at any of these academies, various libraries, collections, and so on — similar to Criterion Collection or something like that, but for art videos. A proto-Patreon or Substack, if you think about it. There's a direct lineage. Lauren Boyle and Marco Roso, co-founders of this, also happen to be on the advisory board for *Do Not Research*, I should mention.

In addition to that, we're going to do a profile on the artist Josh Kline, who was maybe the generation of people before me who was talking about some of these topics but didn't have the unique experience of social media. We're trying to set up a canon and a lineage where you can look at a multi-decade exploration of these thoughts. I think of Josh Kline's work "Forever 27," his explorations into social media, and this incredible show he did in 2013 at 47 Canal. His work is an enormous inspiration and extremely relevant. When you show it to young people who are now making work, they're not, "This is some old person's stuff I need to learn about because the professor said it's important and I want to get a job in this industry later." They're like, "Josh Kline is sick. This thing is really important and relevant." He just did a show called, I mean, you can't—I can't make this up—he did a show called "Climate Change" at L.A. MoCA, and then, a week after the show went down, all of L.A. is enflamed and all of the vegetation has just been burned up in this historically unprecedented fire.

The degree to which the canon of artists that we're looking at was producing work that was immediately relevant to how politics, aesthetics, and culture were shaping the world — those are the things that you try to preserve through the institutional structure. They are worthy of resources being stewarded forward into the future. Future generations care about them, and for good reason. I would also highlight lastly in this, there's a formative exhibition by Susanne Pfeffer called "Speculation on Anonymous Materials," which I believe happened in 2014 at the Frederica Arnhem, I think it's in Kassel, Germany, if I recall correctly. there's a series of exhibitions that kind of group together this cohort of artists that were straddling post-internet and the generation before. We will probably look at that and maybe discuss that in a Josh Kline profile also. But yes, we take this canon-building thing seriously, and I think it's necessary.

Morgane: What would a sustainable platform look like when considering critical and creative practice outside mainstream institutions? And you partially already answered this, but is the idea of building an alternative institution the goal? I mean, I'm very curious to see what the future will bring in terms of *Do Not Research* and all of these other institutions that we see being built, but to what extent and under what conditions are they sustainable, right?

Joshua: Well, sustainable encompasses a few different things. Sustainability necessitates that you have uninterrupted access to publishing on all the different platforms. Substack is, I think, the best right now in terms of upholding things that may get flagged, moderated terms of service, whatever, on any other platform. Substack has the widest Overton window. Of all the posts that we've put up hundreds of them, there are maybe three that we decided not to post because it would risk the violations acts if it was posted in some uncensored capacity. There are limits to it. There's a piece by Eva and Franco Martinez, which was shown at the K.W. Museum in Berlin and could physically be hung on the wall of the museum. We could not put that on to Substack. We could not upload the image because of some of the content in there. Specifically, it is examples given to content moderators of all of the things that you're not allowed to post on social media. It's just a very high-contrast example there. Other things include works that may be sexually explicit that you could see in a gallery context, but if you put them on the internet, they must inevitably become pornography. We have passed a handful of things, but Substack is, for whatever it's worth, the best practical alternative for publishing and hosting at this moment, the harder-to-solve question is the financials of how you make an institution sustainable.

The way that this works now and as it has worked, is that I have a private business in which I just steal time from whatever I'm doing to build this life raft of the institution that I care about, because the amount of time that has to go into this, you can't ask people for 3 to 4 years of unpaid labor. There's just a lot of elbow grease that goes into it. I think of this as legitimacy in itself is important to build. What are you out here arguing for? What is the proposal you have? What is the alternative? At some point, I'm happy to foot a lot of the volunteer labor.

What I hope will happen, which I think we are on track for, is that by year five of *Do Not Research*, there will be a level of crowdfunding that is sufficient to pay one person a part-time salary to just manage the online publication aspects of it. That doesn't bring you an institution overnight. But there are more humble examples of this where people started free message boards and listservs and things that were just internet communities. And then within the course of, five years, they became parts of museums and encountered funding and got grants and all of these things.

That's why we're doing the 501C3 status because it is just not sustainable to operate on volunteer labor. It's just it's hitting levels that are not going to be possible. Having 5A1C3 status allows you to apply to grants to get project-specific funding, to bring people on staff to have someone on a low salary to just, edit the schedule, the publishing handle, the fulfillment of books and just all of the kind of components that go into running this thing that would be indispensable at this point. I feel rather confident that that will happen probably within the next year. Right now, it's just survival at the minimum capacity until we can get across that finish line. I feel optimistic about it, but I constantly am thinking of the sustainability question and the ability to bring in resources without handing over the direction of your institution to the people with the money.

You want to take the best aspects of the platform where you have accountable work and respond to the actual audience that reads the work and cares about it, but you want to avail yourself of the possible resources so that you're not subject to the attention economy. If you can bring in some amount of donor money, maybe split it 50/50, maybe it's, one-third donor, two-thirds crowdfunding. You can shave off the worst aspects of the attention economy, but still retain your autonomy from the donors. Finding that precise mix is something that we're drafting now in the bylaws for how to continue the institution going forward. A lot of these places that exist now take exclusively donor money. They don't know what their analytics are or their traffic. They don't know how many people read their stuff. No one is paying attention to it. They're publishing to an audience of no one. They're publishing work that people don't care about, and it's just entirely captured by the reputational interests of a few wealthy people.

I don't care about making something like that. I've never been good at holding my tongue at a table full of rich people. I'm just happier talking on a podcast and publishing things that people appreciate. Hopefully at some point this year there are enough small donors on Substack and a few people who have money that care enough to contribute to the nonprofit that will make it into a more sustainable model. That does require me to do volunteer work every week for the past four years. But that's where we are. But you know what? We're doing it. We're building the alternative. You also were an early contributor to *Do Not Research.* We've been involved in this for several years and actively thinking about these things. I have I have faith that it will continue.

The Internet Researcher as a Girl Online with Alex Quicho and Sophie Publig

Alex: I'm Alex Quicho, a theorist and research director. My work includes critical writing, performative lectures, and moving images to explore how emerging technologies intersect with our social reality. I'm probably best known for an ongoing project called *Girl Stack,* which collects both extreme and everyday evidence of inhuman girl intelligence and its secret planetary impact.

Sophie: My name is Sophie Publig, and I refer to myself as an internet archaeologist. I'm a senior scientist and postdoc at the Peter Weibel Institute for Digital Cultures at the University of Applied Arts in Vienna. My background is primarily in art history, and now I focus on critical research on memes, digital occultism, and the Anthropocene. I'm interested in unearthing the relationships between nature, culture, and technology, all from a digital culture perspective.

Morgane: I want to begin by asking if you identify with the media figure of the "Girl Online." If so, to what extent do you incorporate this performativity and strategy into your research and publishing practices?

Alex: Well, I suppose my central thesis for *Girl Stack* is that everyone is a girl online. So, yes, I do identify with it. In terms of how I see it and theorize it, the core of my "girl theory" is that platform dynamics encourage people to adopt a girl subjectivity that is inhuman, not necessarily tied to any one body or gender. A significant part of this is related to attractiveness and attentional dynamics, as well as how humans and machines interact, learn from each other, and perceive things like personality, appeal, and magnetism. These qualities are constructed and rewarded within a platform ecosystem. From a personal standpoint, I'm not very strategic about it. I view my online engagement more as a fun, fictional endeavor. I'm trained in critical writing, particularly narrative theory, so I would say my online practice is more aligned with that than with something like performance or systems manipulation. However, these themes are always present in the background of my thinking.

Sophie: I completely agree with what Alex said. I would also identify as a Girl Online, seeing it as a form of practice or a pattern of behavior. It's much more about how you engage with others online, but also, of course, with the platforms themselves. How do you present yourself? How do you showcase your research and the outcomes of what you're doing? And, to some extent, how do you "sell" it? There's already a significant difference between traditional academia, with its journal-industrial complex, and how you actually perform as a researcher online.

Morgane: How has this performativity been used or manifested in the delivery of theory and research? What does this incorporation of performative, nice digital elements add to the publishing of research?

Alex: That's a great question. To put it simply, I'd say it's about pragmatism and respect. Respect for the fact that existing on a platform is not just a 1:1 projection of how you might be in real life. It's also a form of content creation — you're making something, generating something, and putting it into the world. As a result, you also need to respect your audience. By "respect," I don't mean you have to like everyone, but you should recognize that the audience's existence is a factor in your practice.

I'm pretty Instagram- and TikTok-centric, so I think a lot about visual representation. I'm trained in visual art, so I'm accustomed to thinking about things cohesively. I always say that when you create a piece of work, you're no longer making everything from scratch. You're working with pre-rendered assets, which can be both visual and theoretical. When I talk about the "girl," she's a pre-rendered asset in theory — a maximizer, an intensifier of many things. By invoking her, you're already positioning the audience in a space of understanding or contrast.

When you use visual elements in your work or engage with a social platform and its preexisting rules, there are ways to play with these elements. You can engage with things like attraction, seduction, and deception — mechanisms that are already embedded in how people interact with these platforms. These elements don't necessarily work against your work; rather, you can use them to your advantage. It's not about social media marketing, but about being genuinely interested in the medium you're using and understanding that your research is appearing there. It's not just about taking a screenshot of a paper; it's about thinking, "What can I represent well using the tools I have?" and how can I present it in a way that works within the economy of the platform?

Morgane: Sophie, you work as a senior researcher in academia, so on paper, there's not much that forces you to take this step forward and to use strategies like performativity. But as you are a girl online, you do engage in that. I'd also be curious to know how you see this shift impacting the reception of your work.

Sophie: I'd like to build on what Alex was saying. The question of the audience is definitely central. When you publish a conventional academic paper, it can feel like you're shouting your message into the ether, right? Of course, academic work does have a specific audience, but the engagement is much less direct and immediate compared to social media platforms, for example. To effectively navigate the attention economy and reach your target audience, you have to work with aesthetics. You need to find a language that speaks to people — one that's not only engaging but also more inclusive and accessible.

    That's a big part of my personal research approach and how I try to present my work. It's very different from traditional academia in that sense. So, in that regard, aesthetics and language are key for me personally.

Morgane: Do you see your work reaching a different audience when it's packaged in this way, compared to the initial audience, which, in your case, would be the academic researchers who might have engaged with it through traditional channels?

Sophie: Yes, definitely, because the audience on social media platforms is different from the readers of journals behind paywalls. I've also experienced that, on various platforms, you can reach people outside of academia — something that wouldn't happen if you stuck to traditional publishing methods. In that sense, networking on social media is much more specific and also more useful because it reaches people who are actively looking for that kind of content. And since it's much easier to connect with them, there are fewer barriers to collaboration, making it easier to work together.

Morgane: Do you have any self-reflection on this particular strategy or critical insights? Do you see any potential alternatives?

Alex: I don't see this as necessarily a new development. As I mentioned, I'm probably less institutional than some of the other guests on this podcast, but my background is primarily as a writer. When you learn to write, you're always thinking about how to reach an audience and how to popularize an idea. Even when you're dealing with something niche or esoteric, you're constantly considering communication styles and how your message will be received by a specific audience — whether it's an entire country reading a national magazine or a specific subculture engaging with a scene you're circulating. That's always been a consideration.

In that sense, I don't see it as particularly individualistic, unless you want to argue that all authors are bourgeois, idealistic, and individualistic, which, sure, you could make that argument. But I also don't think that's the case because, as anyone who's been to art school knows, authorship is never entirely individual. Everything comes from somewhere else, and ideas flow through you within a lineage of other thinkers. If you have a peer group, they're also influencing how you think and shape the discourse around what you represent.

Social media, in this context, is just an amplifier, as people would traditionally describe it. Around 2016, people talked about the democratic dynamics of social media, which is obviously a lie. In reality, things are amplified in much stranger, more mercenary ways, often tied to forms of representation that don't necessarily have much to do with the ideas themselves. That's an interesting challenge — one that doesn't necessarily serve everyone, and it's not easy to engage with properly. By participating, you're surrendering to certain rules and expectations that often place your face and body center stage, because the algorithm prioritizes visual content. The more you post your face and body, the more visible you'll be.

That's the key distinction: you have to present your ideas in a way that fits within those parameters. From a gender perspective, we might argue that this pressure has always been there for female writers. It's a bit of a boring argument, but I think it's an interesting one in the context of your research.

Sophie: I think this is where the idea of being a Girl Online becomes really interesting — because it's not very individualistic. When we perform as girls online, we're tapping into a collective mindset that many people already have about what it means to be a girl online. As I mentioned earlier, this concept is often cutesy-coded, or very much in line with Tumblr girl blogging, with its specific aesthetics and language. In that sense, we're masquerading in this imagery, which allows us to become more of a person in that context.

What's fascinating is that to engage with this audience, you almost have to "cosplay" a bit — slip into this persona to connect with people who engage with it or even to slip into the algorithm itself. As Alex mentioned, the algorithm prioritizes certain posts, especially image-heavy posts. From there, you can post your opinions, research, or work. So, in a way, you're borrowing from this aesthetic to make your point, to be heard.

This is where the collective versus individual dichotomy collapses. It's something that interests me because it gives this almost automatic sense of community — a feeling of speaking the same language among the girls online. This, in turn, becomes valuable for further collaboration. So, yes, this practice completely differs from traditional academic publishing methods.

Morgane: Do you feel responsible for sharing and making your research available on mainstream platforms beyond academics?

Alex: I'm not sure about responsibility, but I'm highly aware of the concept of "hemispherical stacks" — a term from Bratton — and that what might seem broadly applicable on the internet can be quite region-specific. For example, I see a huge regional difference when I return home, and none of this discourse matters. That's not to say that broader internet discourse isn't important, but how people use certain memes or shorthand to signal and build shared discourse can vary radically depending on traditional nation-state boundaries.

I'm not necessarily responsible for this, but I am deeply aware of it. Even if something circulates on the same platform, it doesn't always translate smoothly into a different region's discourse, especially regarding how networked, individuated culture looks and how it impacts society, politics, and culture.

In that sense, the question of reaching beyond academic spheres is really about attainability and translatability. And that's a challenge I haven't fully figured out. I find myself jumping between different discourse styles depending on where I am and acknowledging that. Education plays a role in this, of course, but it's a challenge to scale globally in terms of how ideas are delivered and how people relate to concepts like the subject, the individual, and the collective.

I don't assume that if I develop a theory about how things happen online, it's going to be universally applicable. So, there's a constant tension between specialization and popularization. Anyone working online has to navigate this challenge because, by existing in that space, there's an implicit expectation that your work should reach a broader audience outside of your immediate institutional sphere. The question then becomes: What's miscommunicated or lost? What needs to be translated, and how do you contend with these expectations? But, honestly, I don't have an answer yet.

Sophie: I think that's a much-needed reality check, especially for academics, and what you're pointing to is crucial. I come from a very traditional background, especially in art history, which is a very conservative discipline. Back when I was studying, I did a lot of higher education activism and institutional critique against universities because the limitations of the discipline are so restrictive. In art history, much of the discourse doesn't even reach the internet in many parts, which is a huge problem. That kind of isolation keeps things within the ivory tower of academia, which automatically makes it seem irrelevant, especially if you're interested in popular culture or digital culture.

There's definitely a need to go outside the academic bubble and use different channels and platforms if you want to stay current. I've always been very interested in how people use the internet and culture, not just in terms of lineages of thinkers or philosophical traditions. Those things certainly play a role, but do they help us with things like Web 2.0 or what we're experiencing today? So much has changed, and while having a theoretical background in culture studies or philosophy is valuable, it doesn't necessarily prepare you for understanding the internet. The only way to learn about the internet is by engaging with it, which many theorists or traditional academics neglect. They tend to focus on reading everything or researching everything, but they miss the point that theory becomes practice.

It's a different way of gathering information — by actually being online and engaging with it. I like to use the somewhat outdated term "netnography" for this because it's important to engage with the smaller ecosystems of different platforms and communities to understand how media-specific the discourse online is to the internet itself.

In that regard, I think it can certainly be an asset. But I often feel like people who are writing about the internet are *chronically online* because it gives a certain authenticity to their work. So it's a two-way street, I guess.

Alex: To add, since you asked for some personal anecdotes, I realize my last answer was a bit abstract. But to be honest, you quickly come up against the difference between mainstream and institutional discourse. For example, I mostly publish in magazines now, and I haven't published in an academic venue since I was an undergrad — that was my last journal publication. I distinctly remember when my first Girls Online article was published in *Wired* magazine, which has millions of readers. It obviously took off in a good way, but I immediately had to confront a lot of hate that I don't think you necessarily encounter on the same scale within institutions. Institutions are generally more conducive to productive dialogue and generative spaces for conflicting or heterogeneous ideas, whereas *Wired* has a very specific audience: people interested in technology, usually with a positive view of it, often male-dominated, and often focused on gadgets and things like when AGI (Artificial General Intelligence) is going to happen.

Wired has a long history of putting certain ideas out into the world and getting them in front of powerful people in the tech industry — economically and infrastructurally speaking. When the *Girls Online* essay was published, it was met with a lot of hatred. People were sending me messages ripping me to shreds, saying things like, "This is incoherent verbal diarrhea" or, "I'm surprised this was written by a woman." Others were asking, "Bro, have you even read Hegel?" It's that kind of harsh critique.

So, when you engage with mainstream publications, people love to criticize traditional publishing, but the readership is still massive. You immediately see how ideas outside of their tight-knit circles can be eaten alive. But I think that's also a good thing. If something is received in that way, it shows not only where its vulnerabilities lie but also where its power is activated. If it's making certain communities feel unstable or angry, maybe it's working in the way it's supposed to.

Morgane: I see how this could happen. This is one of the reasons Carmen Lael Hines and I started the *Girl Employee Podcast* — we realized that, as you mentioned, most people who review or criticize technology are men, and we thought, "This has to change!" But as you rightly pointed out with your anecdote, that's also the main audience that pushes back if you have an opinion. I hope we're seeing a generational shift, where more non-male voices are invading this space, and maybe in 50 years, it won't be such a big issue anymore. But right now, it seems that any critical internet researcher who displays any form of *Girl Online* performativity is easily attacked for having an opinion.

Alex: One of my secret projects is to take a lot of male-coded infrastructural theory and feminize it. But even when you engage on their level, there's still a lot of suspicion from everyone — I guess it's internalized misogyny. If you present things in a girly aesthetic or use certain elements to popularize ideas for a specific audience, it can still be placed in a silo that's unreachable by, quote-unquote, "real" technology critics or people who take the discourse seriously. Practically speaking, it's incredibly backward.

I think a lot of these people are aware of cyberfeminism and the contributions of women to the development of the internet and networks, but in practice, if you represent these things in a way that deviates from a more traditional technological critique — even if you're using the same references — and frame them around how girls online innovate representation, sociability, and communication within the network, it can still be completely dismissed. Not just vilified, but dismissed as inconsequential, as fashion or trend reporting, or just the surface of culture.

I'm not a hater, I'm a fan, but it's an interesting dynamic. The work becomes popularized, but it's also very noticeable who immediately refuses to engage with it. This is, again, a secret project that I think we share, but it's not easy. You can see the barriers in practice when you start putting your work out there and committing to certain styles for their appearance. Those same styles can become a hindrance to its circulation beyond the "girl ecosystem." Misogyny is alive and well.

Sophie: Definitely. I love it when you say you're feminizing infrastructural studies because that's exactly it — that's the process. It also reminds me of something I often hear as a criticism when I, or my collaborators, discuss "girl online" in workshops or talks. The most common criticism usually comes from men, and they'll always ask, "How do you deal with being on commercial platforms? How do you deal with capitalizing on your research?" This criticism often suggests that research or theory should remain pure and untainted by commercialization.

And when I get this criticism, I'm like, yes, you're getting there, but now you need to follow through. For me, "girl online" is just an extension of the cyborg idea, which is all about holding contradictions together. The process of being a girl online is about navigating the contradiction of how to make content or produce "truth" while engaging in this very attention-driven economy of late capitalism. It's a contradiction because, ideally, we like to believe that we're above that — that we don't need to comply with capitalist infrastructure to produce valuable knowledge or research. But the truth is, that's the reality we're in.

Acknowledging that and finding ways to deal with it is much more valuable than just performing the same critique of capitalism over and over. It's inescapable now. Especially if you're using platforms for your research, you can't escape it. Personally, I've decided that I'd rather walk through the contradiction than resort to open-source channels or traditional publishing methods, which are also capitalist in nature. Engaging with users on mainstream platforms, for me, seems like the more honest way to deal with things.

And I think that's something a lot of people who identify as girls will immediately understand. A lot of people who hold on to the "there's no ethical consumption under capitalism" paradigm don't want to engage with it, but to me, that's a denial of the reality we're in. I think this is the crux of the criticism — it's not something to be resolved; it's about engaging with the process.

Morgane: Do you think the topic of critical internet research itself challenges knowledge-making, and if so, for the better or for the worse?

Sophie: I think good research always challenges its own foundations, right? It challenges the very foundations of the discipline. And that's the big project of interdisciplinary research — how much can we stretch boundaries across fields? Not just by producing something new, but by looking at things from different perspectives, which, of course, always leads to the creation of something new.

Alex: I find this question really interesting. A friend of mine once said, "Yeah, when I tell people that we're both chronically online, the other person gets offended. No one wants to admit to having more than five hours of screen time, even though we all do." When you said that, I thought, "I'm not really an internet researcher, I'm not that online," but then I realized, it's all relative.

But, to take it more seriously: I agree with Sophie. All research and cultural production should challenge the present regimes of knowledge production and analysis. That's the point of it. I see a lot of parallels between the femme or "girl side" of the internet and feminist literature. A lot of feminist literature that is prized through a feminist lens reconsiders the subject, error, cohesion, the gap, the attempt, and the essay. There are long intellectual histories about approaching something as an amateur, as an autodidact, or as someone who has to work outside of the traditional, respectable disciplines. Sometimes, the tools available actually fail the ideas you're trying to express. You may have to invent new methodologies to access what you're trying to articulate.

That's why it's hard for me to understand the clear distinctions between different spheres of knowledge production. For instance, we're having this interview in an arts institution. Since we were born, arts institutions have become places for post-disciplinary studies or "deviant research." People are drawn to these institutions not necessarily to produce concise, representational artworks, but because their styles of

147

research are best sustained here in a world that still values qualifications at a certain level. A YouTube video essayist might share methodologies with an art student, for example. There's a lot of overlap between these worlds that isn't necessarily antagonistic. It's about designing new forms of research to answer new kinds of questions. That's where the challenge you're describing exists, but I think it's always part of how we understand, or how we think about understanding, our increasingly complex world.

Sophie: I think this is such a valuable point, especially for the kind of research we're engaging with. I couldn't do the kind of media ecology work I'm doing anywhere else but art school. I tried doing it at traditional universities or within traditional academia, but it just doesn't grasp it. I'm a huge believer that the methods you use should always be in a recursive relationship with the content you're observing. If there's no inherent connection between them, you're probably using the wrong methodology.

When you're looking at the internet, and being chronically online, that connection is essential. I think this is where cultural science really comes through, being interested in the mundane and the things that are often overlooked. Traditional research always looks for exceptions, for something special, out of the ordinary. But it's far more interesting to explore how we engage with things in our daily lives. Maybe that's just a boring form of chronicling, but it's crucial to make sense of what's happening around us.

How it all builds up is what matters. It doesn't matter so much where your methods come from, because, in the end, you're just doing a collage, picking and choosing what works. And that's what you're doing, Morgane, too — combining interviews, research, personal anecdotes, and different methods to reflect the topic you're exploring. So, being chronically online becomes a method, in a sense. It's fun, but it also comes with challenges, like when your private and work lives collapse into one. I use the same Instagram account for my research and personal life, and things overlap. It can be confusing, but it brings us back to embracing contradictions, right? Maybe these polarities are outdated when it comes to something as all-encompassing as the internet.

Morgane: You, Alex, teach in an art school and give lectures. I'm finishing my master's degree in an art school. I think we already come from this hybrid style of research and presenting research. Do you think these are the most optimal spaces for this kind of research, or could it also happen somewhere else in a different way?

149

Alex: I think the variety of ways in which this research happens actually benefits it. Art schools are one place, for the reasons we've discussed. But I also like that there are smaller nodes within larger institutions that can do more inventive work, like the Peter Weibel Institute at the University of Applied Arts where Sophie works,, for example, or places like the New Center for Research or the Institute for Postnatural Studies. These are places that want to reinvent how we think about technology and the philosophy surrounding it.

Institutes within larger institutions, or think tanks, have more licenses to fund and develop critical internet research than you might expect from traditional institutions. I like the idea of these being benevolent parasites within the larger body, pushing discourse into areas it needs to go. But these aren't the only places; what I like about them is that they formalize and support the work financially, something that might be harder for emerging content creators to achieve in an extremely saturated space.

The relationship between institutional and anti-institutional forces remains strong but weird, especially with things like institutional critique. Many large institutions, like the one I teach at (UOL), are highly commercialized, and I don't see much difference between my work life there and how it looked in a corporate research agency. These institutions may produce knowledge like trend research, forecasting, or digital forensics, and they operate like commercial entities. I think the hybrid, monstrous research entity will only grow in importance, and the distinction between institution and commercial independent work will become even less distinct.

Sophie: In Austria, academia is largely privatized but still depends on public funding. When I'm employed in an institution, I see it as an opportunity to have the freedom to do whatever I want with a regular paycheck. However, in Austria, you still need a connection to an institution for funding. As much as I'd love to work independently, it seems necessary to maintain ties to traditional research structures to make a living. For this reason, I still find the institutional link necessary, at least for now.

In art schools specifically, this offers more freedom to experiment with research and explore directions both online and offline. I hope this model can expand in the future, even though I agree with Alex that things might become more commercialized, making it harder to sustain independently. We'll see how it plays out.

Morgane: Thank you so much for this insightful conversation. It's a great conclusion to my research and all the discussions I've had with Joshua and Geert. I'm excited about the future of critical internet research, online girl blogging, and institutional thinking. I look forward to seeing how collaboration continues to evolve. I'm so glad you both spoke with me—your perspectives have been incredibly inspiring for this project.

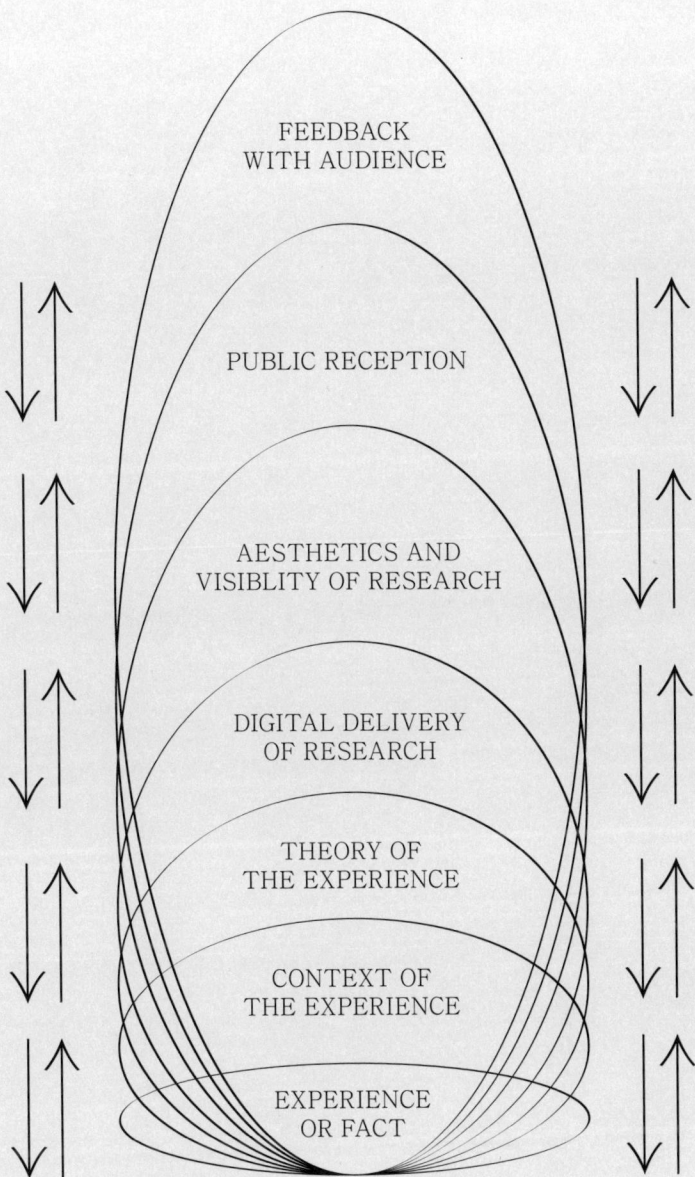

FEEDBACK
WITH AUDIENCE

PUBLIC RECEPTION

AESTHETICS AND
VISIBLITY OF RESEARCH

DIGITAL DELIVERY
OF RESEARCH

THEORY OF
THE EXPERIENCE

CONTEXT OF
THE EXPERIENCE

EXPERIENCE
OR FACT

POSSIBLE FEEDBACK LOOK FOR CRITICAL
INTERNET RESEARCHERS

BIBLIOGRAPHY

Abrams, Loney. "New Artist Strategies, Pt. 1: Can the Subscription-Based Model of the Music Industry Fix the Art World?" *Art Space*, October 27, 2018. https://www.artspace.com/magazine/interviews_features/in_depth/new-artist-strategies-part-1-what-can-the-art-world-learn-from-the-subscription-based-model-of-the-55720.

Arkenbout, Chloe. "The Academic Value of Bottom-up Knowledge Produced by Marginalized Groups: The Relevance of Instagram Infographics for Ethical Terminology Frameworks." *Master of Media UVA*, Webpage, October 3, 2021. https://mastersofmedia.hum.uva.nl/2021/10the-academic-value-of-bottom-up-knowledge-produced-by-marginalized-groups-the-relevance-of-instagram-infographics-for-ethical-terminology-frameworks/?fbclid=IwZXh0bgNhZW0C-MTAAAR0FmTljuJs0g52MI2qVcZ8w73buKdYjDA1lbujlVqNl-iiqv1T9kSghmHpw_aem_3klujBloPAFqOnDB7NU8ug.

Barbrook, Richard. *The Internet Revolution: From Dot-Com Capitalism to Cybernetic Communism.* Network Notebook #10. Amsterdam: Institute of Network Cultures, 2015.

Becker, Howard. *Art Worlds.* University of California Press, 1982.

Bollmer, Grant, and Katherine Guinness. *The Influencer Factory: A Marxist Theory of Corporate Personhood on YouTube.* Stanford University Press, 2024.

Brook, Orian, Dave O'Brien, and Mark Taylor. "'There's No Way That You Get Paid to Do the Arts': Unpaid Labour Across the Cultural and Creative Life Course." *Sociological Research Online* 25, no. 4 (December 1, 2020): 571–88. https://doi.org/10.1177/1360780419895291.

Brown, Symeon. *Get Rich or Lie Trying*.
Atlantic Books, 2023.

Bruce Fleming. *Academia versus the World Outside*.
190: Routledge, 2024.

Citarella, Joshua. "Auto-Experiment: Hyper-Masculinity."
Subscription-based platform. *Patreon* (blog),
September 8, 2021.
https://www.patreon.com/posts/auto-experiment-55888347.

"Commodification." *In Cambridge Dictionary*.
Accessed December 12, 2024.
https://dictionary.cambridge.org/dictionary/english/
commodification.

Consalvo, Mia, and Charles Ess, eds. *The Handbook of
Internet Studies*. Blackwell Publishing, 2011.

David Bolter, Jay. *The Digital Plenitude : The Decline of Elite
Culture and the Rise of New Media*. The MIT Press, 2019.

"Dead Internet Theory: Most of the Internet Is Fake." Forum.
Agoraroad, January 5, 2021.
https://forum.agoraroad.com/index.php?threads/
dead-internet-theory-most-of-the-internet-is-fake.3011/.

Do Not Research. "Do Not Research." Substack,
December 22, 2024.
https://donotresearch.substack.com/.

Eliran Bar-El. *How Slavoj Became Zizek*.
University of Chicago Press, 2023.

Geert Lovink: A Short History of MoneyLab.
Youtube link, 2023.
https://www.youtube.com/watch?v=WIaeWqmyqTE.

Girl Employee. "Girl Online with Sophie Publig."
Accessed December 22, 2024.
https://open.spotify.com/episode/5DUrPe8OFGM-
31MHEMTBkDD?si=m57qnTe4R8yLq_ONa0M1ug.

Hajdakov, Iveta, and Morgan Williams. "I Pick My Poison":
Agency and Addiction in the Age of Subscriptions."
Stripe Partners, 2024.

Hebert, Simon. *Designing Organizations for an Information-
Rich World.* Vol. Computers, Communications, and the
Public Interest. Johns Hopkins Press, 1971.

Hunsinger, Jeremy, Matthew M.Allen, and Lisbeth Klastrup,
eds. *Second International Handbook of Internet Research.*
Springer, 2020.

Jacques Rancière. *History, Politics, Aesthetics.*
Duke University Press Books, 2009.

Kristen, Bateman. "Academia Lives — on TikTok."
The New York Times, June 30, 2020.
https://www.nytimes.com/2020/06/30/style/dark-academia-
tiktok.html.

Lanigan, Roisin. "Nobody Wants to Go to College Anymore."
I-D, November 2, 2021.
https://i-d.co/article/college-admissions-university-decrease/.

Lorusso, Silvio. *Entreprecariat.* Onomatopee, 2019.

Lovink, Geert. *Dark Fiber: Tracking Critical Internet Culture.* The MIT Press, 2003.

Extinction Internet. Institute of Network Cultures, 2022.

"Join the Facebook Exodus on May 31!" Blog. *Institute of Network Cultures* (blog), May 27, 2010. https://networkcultures.org/geert/2010/05/27/join-the-facebook-exodus-on-may-31/.

"Portrait of the Virtual Intellectual." Mailing list. *Nettime* (blog), July 20, 1997. nettime.

Marenko, Betti. "Algorithm Magic: Gilbert Simondon and Techno-Animism." In *Believing in Bits: Digital Media and the Supernatural*, edited by Simone Natale and Diana Pasulka, 0. Oxford University Press, 2019. https://doi.org/10.1093/oso/9780190949983.003.0013.

Memes vs. Museums: Joshua Citarella, Dena Yago, Cem A., G. Quack – The Future of Critique. Youtube Video, 2022. https://www.youtube.com/watch?v=nxFNYaw9LVs.

Miekus, Mela, and Mita Medri. "Silly Girl Theory: Scrolling the Digital Playgrounds." Blog. *Institute of Network Cultures* (blog), February 16, 2024. https://networkcultures.org/longform/2024/02/16/silly-girl-theory-scrolling-the-digital-playgrounds/.

Monoskop. "Institute of Network Cultures." Organization, May 19, 2015. https://monoskop.org/Institute_of_Network_Cultures.

No One Wants to Go to College Anymore.
Youtube Video, 2024.
https://www.youtube.com/watch?v=QzzRsgg5Ccc.

Polyester. "The Girl Is a Living Currency -
How Womanhood Has Always Been Its Own Economy."
Polyester. Accessed December 22, 2024.
https://www.polyesterzine.com/features/the-girl-is-a-living-currency-how-womanhood-has-always-been-its-own-economy.

Quicho, Alex. "Everyone Is a Girl Online."
Wired, September 11, 2023.
https://www.wired.com/story/girls-online-culture/.

Radder, Hans, ed. *The Commodification of Academic Research.* University of Pittsburgh Press, 2010.
https://doi.org/10.2307/j.ctt7zw87p.

Robey, Austin, and Severin Matusek, eds.
After the Creator Economy. Metabel Squad, 2024.
Rogers, Richard. *Digital Methods.* The MIT Press, 2013.

Roth, Emma. "Patreon: Adding Apple's 30 Percent Tax Is the Price of Staying in the App Store." *The Verge,*
August 12, 2024.
https://www.theverge.com/2024/8/12/24218629/patreon-membership-ios-30-percent-apple-tax.

Senay Boztas. "'Culture Is Fragile': Dutch Art World Figures Express Concerns for Future under Potential Coalition Government." *The Art Newspaper,* January 19, 2024.
https://www.theartnewspaper.com/2024/01/19/culture-is-fragile-dutch-art-world-figures-express-concerns-for-future-under-potential-coalition-government.

Strickler, Yancey, Venkatesh Rao, and Maggie Appleton. *The Dark Forest Anthology of the Internet.* The Dark Forest Collective, n.d. Accessed December 22, 2024.

Subsight. "Subsight : Subverting the Attention Economy." Accessed December 22, 2024. https://subsight.netlify.app/theory/.

The Dark Forest Collective || The Dark Forest Anthology of the Internet Roundtable. Youtube Video, 2024. https://www.youtube.com/watch?v=QoyOE-_7dVQ&t=3264s.

University of Queensland. "Disclosure of Interests and Management of Conflicts of Interest." Edu. Accessed December 22, 2024. https://research-support.uq.edu.au/resources-and-support/ethics-integrity-and-compliance/research-integrity/disclosure-interests-and-management-conflicts-interest.

W. Said, Edward. *Representations of the Intellectual.* Vintage, 1996.

Why We Can't Read Full Books Anymore. Youtube Video, 2024. https://www.youtube.com/watch?v=7fz-W-jVT1s&t=2279s.

Wikipedia contributors. "Joshua Citarella." In *Wikipédia,* November 11, 2024. https://en.wikipedia.org/wiki/Joshua_Citarella.

Williams, James. *Stand out of Our Light.* Cambridge University Press, 2018.

Colophon

Set Margins' #68

BECOMING THE PRODUCT
The Critical Internet Researcher as a Virtual Intellectual

ISBN 978-90-835325-1-6

Author:
Morgane Billuart

Text editor and proofreader:
Helena McFadzean

Graphic design and illustration:
Juliette Lépineau

Proofreader:
Helena McFadzean

Advisor:
Geert Lovink Set Margins'

Fonts:
Aktiv Grotesk,
Adobe Myungjo Std

Paper:
Maestro print

Printer:
Balto Print

Made possible thanks to
the generous support of:
Goethe Institut
European Union
Hufak
Set Margins'

Funded by
the European Union

GOETHE
INSTITUT

hufʌk

Funded special project of the
Students' Union at the University
of Applied Arts Vienna.

This work was produced with
the financial assistance of
the European Union. The views
expressed herein can in no way
be taken to reflect the official
opinion of the European Union.

Special thanks to friends,
lovers and relatives.

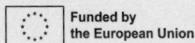

Set Margins'
www.setmargins.press